THE ABBEY

A Story of Discovery

JAMES MARTIN, SJ

HarperOne
An Imprint of HarperCollinsPublishers

For M.

HarperOne

This book is a work of fiction. The characters, incidents, and dialogue are drawn from the author's imagination and are not to be construed as real. Any resemblance to actual events or persons, living or dead, is entirely coincidental.

HarperCollins books may be purchased for educational, business, or sales promotional use. For information please e-mail the Special Markets Department at SPsales@harpercollins.com.

HarperCollins website: http://www.harpercollins.com

IMPRIMI POTEST: Very Reverend John Cecero, SJ

FIRST HARPERCOLLINS PAPERBACK EDITION PUBLISHED IN 2016

Designed by Level C

Illustration by Julia Lonneman

Library of Congress Cataloging-in-Publication Data is available upon request.

ISBN 978-0-06-240213-4

16 17 18 19 20 RRD(H) 10 9 8 7 6 5 4 3 2 1

I

When the baseball crashed through his window, he was thinking about Ted Williams.

Mark had once read that the Red Sox great claimed that when a fastball was screaming toward him at home plate, he could see the stitches on the ball. Mark couldn't see the stitches, but he was aware that the ball was headed directly toward him. A line drive, the radio announcer would say, and he could almost hear the Red Sox games his father listened to during the summer. Back then, June, July, and August seemed like one endless baseball game.

For a brief moment the ball appeared motionless, and then grew larger, like a globe rapidly expanding.

He jumped out of the way just before it crashed theatrically through the glass, smacked the tall maple bookcase behind him as if it were a backstop, knocked out a few yellowing paperbacks, and landed with a demure plop on the carpet.

"Shit!" he said, to no one in particular. He peered through the jagged glass into the neighboring yard. He knew right where to look. It was where they always played ball and made too much noise. The three teenage boys who lived on his block were friendly, but occasionally bothersome.

He spotted them now and called down, "What the hell were you doing?"

"Sorry!" came a trio of adolescent voices. The neighboring yard was several feet lower than his. Mark could never figure out what accounted for the strange undulations in his neighborhood, but some lawns were high, others low. Sometimes he worried about his house being swallowed up by one of those monstrous sinkholes he saw on the news, but it was probably just a natural depression, nothing special. Now it exaggerated his vantage point; from his first-floor glassed-in den, he looked down on the boys as if from a great height.

"It's almost the middle of the night!" he shouted. This was clearly an exaggeration—it was only nine o'clock—but anger made him skate over the error. He repeated himself, more loudly.

"What the hell are you doing playing ball in the middle of the night?" *And who,* he asked himself, *breaks windows with baseballs these days?* He felt as if he were in a 1960s sitcom.

The three boys dragged themselves up the incline and entered Mark's yard. Standing a few yards from his window, they unsuccessfully tried to hide their fascination at the destruction they had caused, as they contemplated the shards of glass sparkling on the dark lawn.

It was odd to see the three boys standing still. Normally, he saw them racing around the neighborhood, either on their bikes or, more recently, in one of their parents' cars. A few days ago he had narrowly missed one of them riding a bike, no-handedly, on the street. But now they were rooted in place, apparently weighed down by guilt. As they inched closer to the broken window, Mark felt his empathy kick in.

"Uh . . . sorry, Mark," one said, looking up. Then he corrected himself: "Mr. Matthews." Their upturned faces made the sixteen-year-olds look younger.

What a dumb name, he thought, not for the first time. Dull to all but religious people who often asked, "Do you have brothers named Luke and John?" Long ago, he had promised himself that when he had children, he would not name them after anyone who wrote a Gospel.

He used to ask women he dated what names they'd pick for their children, which either spooked them or prompted them to think that a ring was forthcoming. So he stopped inquiring. But occasionally, before he dozed off at night, he mused on names for his children. At age thirty, he was starting to worry about whether he'd ever find someone . . .

The three boys stared at him. Mark took a step forward and felt glass crunch underfoot. Tomorrow he would have to tell Anne, his landlady. She'd freak out. So he grew angry again.

"Who's going to pay for this mess?" he asked, sounding like his father. Was there an internal script for these events that his mental hard drive automatically accessed?

"Um . . . us," said Brad, whom Mark considered the group's leader. "Is that okay?"

"Yeah, fine," he said. "Hey, I know it was an accident. I used to do stupid things too. And I know you're all good kids." They brightened at that. One boy smiled in relief, caught himself, and frowned again.

"So," Mark said, "just come back tomorrow, and we'll figure out how much this is going to cost."

"Okay." They dispersed then, in three different directions, one carrying a bat, each with his own glove. The small event was large enough to unsettle them, shatter their evening camaraderie, and drive them homeward.

Mark remembered what Brad's father said after his son passed his driver's test. Mark was washing his car when Brad pulled into the driveway next door, after his long-awaited appointment at the Department of Motor Vehicles. The kid was so excited that he forgot to act cool.

"Mark, I passed!" he shouted through the open window as he honked the horn. "I passed, I passed, I passed!"

Brad got out of the car, slammed the door, flew up the steps to his house, taking two at a time, and threw open the door. "Mom! I passed!"

His father, a heavy man, grinned slyly as he extricated himself from the car.

"Congratulations," said Mark. "Sixteen already, huh? I guess they grow up fast."

"Are you kidding?" said the father. "Longest sixteen years of my life!"

Mark looked out at the darkening yard and heard crickets chirping. *I should probably cover the window with plastic,* he thought, *after I clean up this mess.*

2

As he stretched his rangy body in bed, Mark's first thought was not that it was a Saturday—and that he could rest after having spent so much of the past week sanding and repainting the monastery fence—but that he would have to tell his landlady about the broken window and ask her for the name of a repairman. Anne was a stickler for that.

"If you have to do any kind of repairs," she told him when he first rented the house, "I want to know. And I want to tell you whom to call. I don't want you calling some idiot repairman."

Looking at her levelly, he had willed himself not to remind her that he was an experienced carpenter, not to mention an architect. She seemed to read his mind, something he found both alarming and attractive.

"I know you're a carpenter," she said, "so it's nothing personal. I just like to know the people who are working on the house. I'm sure you can understand."

He nodded politely.

A few hours later, with the sun overhead and the cicadas proclaiming the coming humidity, he made his way to Anne's house, just a few doors away. Mark already felt a kind of ownership of the block, even though he had lived there only a year. "My neighborhood," he liked to say to his friends, something he'd not said since he was a kid in Boston. Built in the late 1950s, the low-slung, split-level brick houses were kept tidy by their owners, mainly young couples with children, empty nesters, and widows. Mark was the rare renter, something that initially incurred not just the curiosity of his neighbors, but also their suspicion. But by doing odd jobs for them—helping one build a stone wall for his garden; helping another perfect his stucco technique; shoveling snow when asked by the elderly ladies, who seemed to hide in their houses except when a job needed doing; and being friendly with the teenage boys, who admired his frequent dates with attractive women—he cemented his place in the neighborhood after a few months.

The street looks its best in the spring, he thought, with the tall maple trees unfurling their pale green leaves, dogwood trees wearing short-lived white flowers, and ornamental cherry trees sporting puffy pink blossoms. Just this week the lilac bushes lining the side of the house had come into light purple bloom. Yesterday, before he left for work, Mark had paused to enjoy the lilac-scented air. The single discordant note was the braying of leaf blowers, weed whackers, and lawn mowers, which crowded out silence on weekends in the spring, summer, and fall.

Anne's house looked like his house; she had made sure of that. The same neatly trimmed yew bushes, the same stone-lined flower beds, and the same tall black lampposts on the front lawns announced to the neighborhood that both number 105 and number 111 were hers. Her ex-husband, Mark had heard, pleaded that the two houses at least be painted different colors. That, apparently, was one of the few battles he had won. So Anne's house was trimmed in red, and Mark's—or rather, Anne's other house—in white.

There was a long oval of clear glass in the center of the front door, so Mark could see into her living room. He gently knocked on the door. "Anyone home?"

Immediately, his landlady's annoying little yap dog, as he called it, tore down the stairs from the second floor, planted himself before the window, and barked frantically. When Mark did not leave, the dog shifted to growling and baring its teeth. While Mark stared down the dog, he examined the reflection of his long, sandy hair. He should probably get a haircut today. *What compels people to buy these little dogs?*

Anne appeared and pulled open the door. "Shut up!" Noting the surprise on Mark's face, she added, "Sorry. This insane dog."

She deftly pushed the dog back with her left foot, opened the screen door, and slipped outside, almost pushing Mark off the concrete steps. Politely, he moved backward and down a step. Now he was roughly at her height.

"Hot!" she said, meaning the day, but she could have meant herself. At forty, Anne looked good. Her light brown hair was pulled back in a no-nonsense style, a few strands hanging over her forehead, and only the faintest lines spider-webbed around her blue eyes. Today she wore gray yoga pants, pink flip-flops, and a green-and-white Eagles T-shirt.

"Yeah," he said. "It's gonna be pretty brutal later on, I think."

"Awful!" she said looking up at the sky. "I hate this humidity. My mom used to call it 'close.' So how are you, Mark? Still doing the work those men should be doing for themselves?"

When Mark had first met Anne and described his job at the monastery, Anne reacted strongly. "Painting, raking leaves, fixing pipes, and dealing with plumbing is something that men should be able to do. I do it!" she said.

"It's not that they won't do it," he had said, not wanting to get drawn into a debate. "It's that they can't do *all* of it, and some of them are pretty old. Plus, some of them don't know how. Those guys are great, really great—well, most of them— but put a few of them in front of a hammer and they wouldn't know which end to grab. Now, some of them are incredibly talented with those things. Brother Michael, you know, built a lot of that monastery himself. In fact, he designed the guest house and . . ."

"Right," she had said, looking annoyed.

Mark wanted to defend the monks, but then remembered why he came, and how she would probably be even more annoyed about the window. Instead, he said offhandedly, "Anyway, I like it at PB&J."

She stared at him.

"That's what I call it," he said. "You know they make jam there, right?"

"Yes, I know that."

"So they make the jam . . . and their monastery is the Abbey of Philip and James. P&J everyone calls it around here, but I call it PB&J. Peanut butter and jelly? The abbot thinks it's pretty funny."

"Uh-huh." She was looking at him as though trying to figure out how to get him off her step. "So what brings you by anyway?"

"Well, you're not going to like this."

"Now what?"

"Last night some of the kids were playing baseball next door and hit a ball that went right through the back window."

"Jesus Christ," she said, sounding more tired than angry.

"Don't worry," he said. "I can call a glazier—you know, someone who fixes windows."

"Yes, I know what a *glazier* is."

"I didn't mean it like that," he said, flushing again. "It's easy to take care of. There was no damage to the frame. And the kids said they'd pay for it."

"You mean their parents will," she said. "Let me give you the name of the guy I deal with."

When she opened the door, he felt air conditioning brush his bare legs. The yap dog lunged for him, but was blocked by Anne's foot as she stepped inside. The dog barked behind the door as Mark watched Anne rummage through the drawers of a cabinet in her living room. On the walls he could see framed photos of Anne and her friends, and many of her son. One was a class picture; in front of a fake background of light blue sky and puffy white clouds he beamed, wearing a white button-down shirt. With his light brown hair and fair skin, he looked like Anne.

"Here," she said, handing him a business card through the open door. "You can call this guy. He knows what he's doing. Sorry if I'm a little rushed. I have a yoga class later on, and a million other things to do. Everything else okay in the house?" The dog yapped insolently.

"Sure," he said. "And I really like living there."

"Glad to hear it," she said, smiling now. "Enjoy the day. Be cool." She shut the door. He heard her muffled voice: "Shut up you lunatic *dog*!"

As he reached her driveway, the trio of window-breaking boys rolled by on beat-up skateboards, shouting to one another. When they saw Mark, they fell silent, evidently remembering the line drive. But when he waved, their boards crunched to a halt on the sidewalk.

"Hey, Mark," said Brad, who offered his hand. "We'll get that money to you soon." He took Brad's hand and shook it.

The other two, John and Gary, followed suit, offering wordless apologies with outstretched hands. Then they fell into their usual easy banter with him, expressing amazement at how the ball had gone so far and so fast and right into the window. They grew more animated.

"Oh, *man*!" John said. "I couldn't believe it! We were freaking *out* when we saw where it was going! Glad you're cool with it, man."

"No problem, guys," said Mark. "Just be careful."

John raised his eyebrows and looked pointedly at Anne's house.

"Yeah, you too, man!" Mark rolled his eyes, as Gary guffawed. Brad frowned and looked at the ground.

Then they tore off on their boards.

3

As Anne closed the door she thought, *Yes, I know all about the monastery.*

She wished Mark remembered that she had grown up in the area. He was forever telling her things about Philadelphia, as if she were a tourist. When she was a girl, her father used to take her to the Abbey of Saints Philip and James, a Trappist monastery forty-five minutes away, located on acres of secluded land blanketed with pine trees. He used to drag her along to visit an ancient priest with bad breath, who always called her "Annie," though she told her father that no one else called her that.

"Deal with it," he said more than once. "Father Edward can call you anything he wants. He's a holy man, and he's been very good to your mother and me. He made a special trip to our parish to baptize you, remember?"

"Then why doesn't he know my name?" she had asked more than once.

I know all about the abbey, she wanted to say. But she hadn't been on the grounds in years. That part of her childhood, once important, had ebbed away. Mark's work there had prompted her to think about the place for the first time in years.

She knew about the jam too. Her father bought it by the case, and she used to buy it for her son, who never seemed to be able to get enough of the blueberry preserves. "Jeremiah, you're going to turn into a blueberry," she said to him one Sunday morning, after he'd finished three pieces of toast thickly slathered with the preserves. He must have been eight years old.

"Tell me when I turn blue!" he responded. Then he inhaled, puffed out his cheeks crazily, and held his breath until he started laughing.

Thinking of that prompted her to turn toward the photos, framed in gold, on the wall. She still wasn't sure if she should keep them.

She had seen Mark staring at them through the front door. She loved that school photo of Jeremiah; it was her favorite. Everyone said he looked just like her, though she thought he looked more like his father. The blue eyes. The snub nose. And especially that pointy chin.

In the past few months she had thought about removing the photos, not because she couldn't look at them, which she did frequently, but because they seemed to make others feel uncomfortable. When people looked at the photos, they usually glanced furtively over their shoulder, to be sure that their looking wasn't too painful for her.

She noticed a smudge on the glass of the portrait and rubbed it off with her forefinger. The action brought her closer to the image of Jeremiah.

Anne peered into her son's eyes and remembered the argument the two of them had over what he was going to wear on picture day at school. Jeremiah wanted to wear the Phillies T-shirt his father had bought him at the game that summer, but she refused. "You're not wearing a *T-shirt* for your school picture."

During their heated argument, her son, ten at the time, started to cry, a rarity for him. His friend Brad was going to wear his, he pleaded, his voice rising an octave.

"And if Brad jumped off the Walt Whitman Bridge, would you do that too?" She asked that question so often that Jeremiah used to tease her about it.

"Yes!" he said, grinning. Jeremiah's quicksilver mood changes always amazed her.

"I would jump off the Walt Whitman Bridge! Like this," he said, clasping his hands together and forming his slender body into a mock diving position. "*And* I'd be wearing that Phillies shirt while I did it! And on the way down I'd say, 'Go Phillieeeeeees!'" He almost collapsed in laughter. The person who could make Jeremiah laugh hardest was always Jeremiah.

Anne could almost hear his laugh, which was what she missed most about him. Her chest tightened, and tears sprang to her eyes. She thought it not only unfair, but cruel, that she would never hear her son laugh again.

"God damn it," she said aloud, and she felt the familiar hollow in her stomach open up.

Anne inhaled and exhaled deeply as she turned away from her son's photo, willing herself to continue her day.

4

By Monday the window was repaired, to Mark's relief. The glazier (how could he have been so dumb to insinuate that Anne didn't know what that was?) carried a pristine square of glass from his truck and expertly fit it to the window frame. Although Mark was glad to see it fixed, he had also enjoyed the brief novelty of the broken glass, which allowed the humid air to creep into the room as he watched the ball game on Sunday night, enjoying a beer.

The weather remained sticky, even though the sun hadn't shown its face since Sunday afternoon. How could Philly be so humid? Sometimes he felt as if he had moved to Atlanta. Everything south of New England was too hot for him. He pulled out of his driveway, checking to make sure that no boys were screaming down the road on their boards or that Brad wasn't driving his father's car.

The drive to the monastery was an easy one and enjoyable on most days. Out of his neighborhood, up the Blue Route, and past the towns he always wanted to visit, though he never seemed to find the time to do so.

"St. Davids," he once said to John, Brad's father. "What's St. Davids like? Sounds picturesque, like some Welsh mining town."

"Uh-huh," said John. "Try buying a house around there, and you'll see how much the miners' cottages are going for."

Mark turned on the radio and fiddled with the dials, unsuccessfully trying to find a song he liked. He turned off at the exit onto a smaller road. After a year, he knew the route cold. Forty-five minutes door-to-door wasn't so bad; and even if traffic delayed him, the monks didn't care if he was a little late, unless he was scheduled to meet with a contractor. For men whose lives revolved around the clock, they were surprisingly tolerant of his tardiness. Mark had said as much to the abbot, meaning it as a compliment.

"Our lives revolve around God, not the clock," the abbot said.

He liked Father Paul. As head of the abbey, he could have insisted on being called Abbot Paul, but on the first day he told Mark, "I've been Father Paul for so long that it fits."

Abbot came from a word meaning "Father," Mark had discovered in his online research after his first day of work, during which he'd been introduced to a raft of unfamiliar words. When he asked Dave, a college friend who recommended him for the job, if the monks spoke Latin, Dave howled.

"Oh yeah!" said Dave. "That's how I communicate with them when I'm doing their books—in *Latin*. We all speak Latin to one another. Of course they don't speak Latin, you nimrod."

But on that first day they might as well have been. The English words the monks used were ones Mark remembered only dimly from his architectural studies. "Refectory," "cloister," "chapter house" he heard on the first day, as Father Paul showed him around the abbey.

Mark never did, and never would, get the hang of the names of the times that the monks prayed in chapel, which occurred every few hours. With the exception of "Vigils," which made some sense, the terms identifying the other times of prayer—"Lauds," "Compline," "Sext," and "None"—seemed like nonsense words. He had been corrected enough times on the pronunciation of "Compline" ("*Com*-plin, not com-*pline*," said one older monk sourly) that he now simply said, "Your prayers." Why couldn't they just say "morning prayer" or "evening prayer"? Or maybe they intentionally made their way of life inscrutable to outsiders.

After being laid off from his entry-level job at an architectural firm in Cambridge, Mark had spent a few months scrounging around for carpentry jobs in Boston. As a college student he had worked as an apprentice to a local carpenter to help pay for tuition, and he enjoyed the work. During the first few months after the layoff, Mark figured he could make a go of it; he remembered how much he enjoyed the manual labor. But the carpentry work was sporadic at best, and if he wasn't going to default on his massive student loans, he would have to find something more permanent.

So when Dave, who helped the monks with their taxes, told Mark about a full-time job at the monastery, he jumped, even though he would miss Boston. It would be steady work and some carpentry in the suburbs of Philly, which he had heard was a more affordable place to live. He had lived in Cambridge so long that he thought Anne was joking when she quoted the monthly rent on the house.

"You want me to raise it?" she asked when she saw his face.

The first day at the abbey, though, was profoundly weird. He remembered that now as he made a left at the sign that had the word "Monastery" floating above a fat red arrow pointing to a long snaking driveway lined with massive pine trees.

The monastery was built in the 1950s, when suburban towns and villages were blossoming around Philadelphia, as World War II veterans searched for quiet places to settle down with their wives and families. The archbishop of Philadelphia invited the monks to start an abbey here, to "support our growing church with your constant prayers" read the yellowing letter, framed and still hanging in the sacristy.

Mark once remarked to one of the monks that the archbishop of Philadelphia had beautiful handwriting. That kind of round, flowing script was a lost art. "I'll bet he went to Catholic school, and the nuns taught him that!"

"Yes," said Brother Benjamin, irritated, "they did."

Mark's jokes sometimes fell flat with the monks.

The monastery was named after Saints Philip and James not because of any special devotion the monks had for the two, but because they were the favorite saints of the archbishop who invited them to Philadelphia. When Mark learned that James was one of the apostles and called "the Lesser" (instead of another apostle named James, called "the Greater") and that Philip had once doubted that Jesus could perform a miracle, he judged the monastery's name pretty lame, considering there were other, more famous apostles to choose from.

Nearly everyone in the area, even those who weren't Catholic, knew the place—if only for the jam that the monks made to support themselves and that held pride of place in local supermarkets. They called it the Abbey of P&J, or the abbey, or the monastery, or sometimes just P&J. Sometimes, when Mark told women he dated where he worked, they seemed impressed, as if they were meeting a saint. "I'm just the *handyman,* for God's sake," he would say. One woman, however, seemed turned on by it, which creeped him out.

But his architectural soul felt a thrill when he saw the place for the first time. Built in the local stone called Wissahickon schist, a rough gray shale that glittered in the sun, the abbey church was a long rectangular building with a peaked wooden roof and a tall stone bell tower that stood beside it. That was the first thing you saw as you approached the abbey, and he never tired of watching the bell tower rise slowly over the driveway as he drove up the hill. Until his first day there, he had never been inside a monastery, though he had studied them in his class "The Medieval World" in architecture school. If you were paying attention as you drove past on the Blue Route, you could see the tall gray steeple poke above the hilly landscape.

A few minutes before his interview on that fall morning last year, he had opened the heavy wooden door to the church and was almost floored by the sound of chanting, something he had heard only on the radio. *People still sing like this?* His next thought was: *This is the most beautiful thing I've ever heard.*

He found a place in a pew and listened to the rising and falling men's voices, unaccompanied but for a single organ note at the beginning of each stanza. Listening more carefully, he realized that they were singing in English. He didn't know much about Catholicism (neither of his parents went to a church of any kind) and even less about monks and monasteries, but he could tell they were singing psalms.

"Blessed be the name of the Lord," sang one voice. Then the rest answered with other verses. At the end of their prayers, they sang a hymn with an organ accompanying them.

There were only two other visitors in the church on that day—an old woman and a young man—both seated a few pews ahead of Mark. After the chanting stopped, they stood, knelt down and crossed themselves as Catholics do, and exited the church. Both smiled at him on the way out. Before the door closed, he could hear them talking to each other outside, under the portico. Even from the few words he caught, Mark sensed that they were acquainted through their visits here. The old woman's presence he could understand, but what was a college-age kid doing at a monastery at seven in the morning?

Connected to the church was the dormitory, where the monks slept. That part of the abbey included the chapter house, where they gathered for meetings; the infirmary, for the sick monks; and the refectory, where they ate. A few hundred feet away, in a separate building, was the jam factory, where they produced "Monastery Jam," sold locally and through mail-order catalogues and a website. "Jam puts the rest of the food on the table," said Father Paul with a smile.

On that first day Mark wasn't sure where he was supposed to meet the abbot. But Paul found him. Mark stood outside the church lighting up a cigarette when the abbot emerged from a side door.

"I'm Father Paul," he said, offering his hand. "Welcome to the Abbey of Saints Philip and James. You're Mark, I guess?"

Paul had a pale, thoughtful face, large blue eyes, thinning gray hair, and enormous glasses. His handshake was firm, his hand soft—not the hand of someone who did much manual labor. On the plus side, he looked like what Mark's mother used to call a "kind soul."

Mark snubbed out a cigarette on the flagstone pavement under the portico and noticed Paul's face register mild disapproval. Only then did he notice Paul's getup.

"Wow," said Mark, surveying the abbot's long white robe and the heavy black cloth that covered his shoulders and hung down to his knees. (A few months later, Mark found out that the black cloth was called a "scapular.") A thick brown leather belt cinched around his waist completed the monk's outfit.

"Ah, yes," said the abbot. "Welcome to the eleventh century. Our habit is pretty strange, isn't it?"

"No, it's pretty cool," said Mark, meaning it. "Does it have pockets?"

Paul reached into a pocket and pulled out a set of keys that jangled and sparkled in the autumn light. "The keys to the kingdom," he said triumphantly.

"The what?"

"Sorry," said Paul. "An attempt at a joke. Why don't you follow me, I'll show you around, and we can talk about the job. Dave gave you an excellent recommendation." Mark made a mental note to take Dave out for a beer in Philly.

Mark followed the abbot into his office and noticed he was wearing sandals—Birkenstocks—with socks, which gave him a vaguely hippielike air.

The job was not what Mark expected he would be doing at this moment in his life. Back in school he had listed his career goals on a small square of quadrille-ruled paper that he kept tucked in his wallet for a few years. By this point, he was supposed to have founded his own small architectural firm with friends. As Mark found himself farther and farther behind in his ambitions, he finally threw the paper away.

Still, he found that he liked working at the abbey more than toiling behind his desk at the firm, where he had spent most of his time designing bathrooms for office buildings in downtown Boston.

"Director of the Physical Plant" was his title, something the abbot insisted on calling him, even though he felt he was just a handyman. "Don't forget that Jesus was a carpenter," Father Paul said several times during the first month. Mark was busy with many things: painting endless hallways, fixing leaky pipes and toilets that probably had never flushed right, plastering water-damaged walls, raking leaves in the cloister garden, and mowing the largest lawn he had ever seen or ever hoped to see.

Often Mark spent hours supervising contractors the abbot had called to fix something beyond Mark's expertise. A huge complex of buildings built so long ago needed an enormous amount of care. And with only twenty-seven monks, several of them busy in the jam factory and many of them elderly, Mark had plenty to do. Occasionally he even got to do some carpentry. He was particularly proud of a new pine shelf he installed in a side chapel in the abbey church, dedicated to Mary, or "Our Lady," as Father Paul said.

That was almost a year ago. By now Mark felt at home. He liked the monks, most of them at least, and a few days into the job he realized that his initial impression had been wrong. They didn't have such an easy life: rising at insanely early hours, praying all the time, working both inside the house and in the jam factory, and eating extremely simple meals. They took vows of poverty, so none of them owned anything, not even their habits. Lots of fasting during Lent too, he gathered.

Plus, no sex. That part made their lives seem impossible. When one monk asked him in a friendly way if he ever thought of joining them, Mark laughed out loud. The monk was not pleased with this response.

Father Paul had also become a kind of confidant for Mark. He still didn't know many people in Philly other than Dave, whom he saw only occasionally, and whatever women he met in bars in Center City or online. Last summer, Dave invited him to join a local softball league, which turned out to be fun, but most of the guys on the team were either married or on their way to marriage, so invitations to a drink or a ball game meant that either their wives or their girlfriends came along. That ended up making Mark feel even lonelier.

One day, driving home from work, it dawned on him that the person he spent the most time with was Father Paul. He smiled to himself, finding it funny (or bizarre or pathetic, he wasn't sure) that his best friend in Philly, next to Dave, was a monk.

But Paul was a good listener, patient, with a lively sense of humor. Something else Mark appreciated about the abbot: he always seemed calm. Unflappable even when a portion of the ceiling in the jam factory collapsed after a huge snowstorm in December. Paul simply peered up at the gaping hole in the ceiling and down at the sodden acoustical tiles on the factory floor and the plastic yellow bucket that caught the dripping water and said, "Well, that's something, isn't it?"

And no matter what you told Paul, he seldom seemed surprised, much less disturbed. Sometimes Mark wondered how you got to be a person like the abbot—patient, listening, not judging. Open. Mark would complain about a date that had gone bad, a woman who dumped him, or a heated argument he'd had with a contractor, and Paul took it in stride. At times he could even make Mark laugh about some of his problems. Once Mark angrily told him how a woman had thrown a drink in his face the night before, and Paul's first response was, "Did you deserve it?"

Today's work shouldn't be too tough. Finish painting the wall in the refectory that he replastered after last week's storm, install a new shower stall in a bathroom on the second floor of the dormitory, and help Brother Robert unload a shipment of jars for the jam factory.

Brother Robert was another favorite—friendly, quiet, practical, and with a head for business. The monks Mark appreciated most were those who had worked, as they said, "in the world" before entering the monastery. Brother Robert always smiled when Mark called it the "Abbey of PB&J." A few weeks after he started the job, Mark handed him a case of gourmet peanut butter for the community on All Saints Day, which he knew was a big day for them, as a gag gift.

"First time anyone's ever given us a case of peanut butter," said the monk.

"First time I ever knew when All Saints Day was," said Mark.

At the end of the workday, around five, Brother Robert waved at him as he entered the noisy jam factory. Mark assumed it was to check if the jars arrived; they hadn't. Instead, Brother Robert told him he had a phone call.

Who would call me here? he wondered.

Maddy, who worked in the guest house and was visiting Brother Robert, handed him a small pink slip of paper. When Mark first came to the abbey, he was surprised to discover so many of what he called "nonmonks" working in the factory. "There are only twenty or so in the community who are able-bodied," said Brother Robert. "And you don't have to be a monk to make jam."

At first he found Maddy, a seventyish woman with a long, mournful face and a slow gait, which he ascribed to arthritis, distant. She was also overly deferential to the monks. "The holy fathers and brothers" she often called them. Mark knew she was trying to be funny, but he suspected that Maddy *did* think they were all holy. He didn't—he'd seen enough of the monks grow testy when a toilet wasn't fixed on time or irritated when Mark was hammering too loudly. ("It's a hammer," he said to a monk who screwed up his face when he passed Mark fixing a table in the refectory. "It's loud.") The monks could get angry, and even petulant, like anyone else. In time, though, he grew to appreciate Maddy for her work ethic. She was loyal to the monks and the monastery, never late, and always efficient.

"Anne called," said the note. At first he was happy to see the name: a lawyer he met at a crowded bar in Center City last week. But then he saw the phone number: his landlady. Now what? Had the window not been fixed to her exacting specifications?

Stepping outside, he took out his cell phone and punched in her number. The day was getting even warmer, with full, darkening clouds foretelling a thunderstorm.

"Is this Mark Matthews?" she asked before he could say anything. "I'm sorry to call you at work, but I didn't have your cell and I know you work at the monastery." She sounded agitated.

"No problem," he said. "What's up?"

"This is kind of embarrassing, but I was on my way home

from work and I'm stranded. My car broke down in the parking lot, and everyone I work with already left, so I was wondering if you could pick me up on your way home. Is that doable? I'm at the garage where they towed the car, not too far from St. Davids."

"Sure," he said. "Let me get a pencil, and you can tell me how to get there."

"Oh, I have no clue where I am. Let me give the phone to one of the mechanics."

Mark copied down the directions and hung up. "I have to pick up a woman in St. Davids," he said to Brother Robert.

"Well, congratulations," he said.

"No, it's my landlady."

"Oh, condolences then."

5

Anne was standing outside the gas station, waving and smiling. *She looks good,* he thought, with her hair pulled back, wearing a tailored white shirt that showed off her slender figure. He wondered if he should ask her out, and then reminded himself of their age difference. *Still . . .*

"Thank you so much," she said, climbing into the truck. "I feel like an idiot."

"Don't worry about it. Happy to help."

"How's life at Peanut Butter Abbey?" she said. "Isn't that what you call it?"

"PB&J."

"Right," she said flatly. "How was work?"

"Great! I got tons of stuff done today. It's a good feeling to do work and just get stuff done. Cross it off the to-do list, you know?"

"Uh-huh." She sounded distracted.

"How's the car?" he asked.

She exhaled. "Lousy. I freaking hate that car. My ex-husband bought it, and I've never liked it."

Mark knew not to ask about her husband. One evening in the early fall, Brad's father, John, recounted the story, a week after Mark moved into the neighborhood. John was watering his rose-bushes as he did so. They were talking about Mark's dating life.

"How are things with Susie?" asked John. "Is that her name?"

"You mean Nancy? Or Stacy?"

"Who can keep track?" John guffawed. The conversation turned to Mark's hopes for marriage, then to news about other families on the street, and then to Anne.

Anne had grown up not far from the neighborhood and moved into her current house at a young age, along with her husband, who had been her high-school sweetheart. "He was quite the jock," said John. "Played minor league ball at some point, I think." Anne's parents owned her house, and another one on the same street. After they died, she inherited both houses. The extra one, where Mark now lived, had provided her and her husband with some additional income.

A few months after moving in, Anne became pregnant, something that obviously made her happy. After Jeremiah was born, Anne loved pushing him around in his stroller through the neighborhood and waving to all of her neighbors. Some-times she'd sit on the front step of her house reading a paper-back as the baby snoozed on a blue blanket spread out on the lawn under the big maple tree. "She was a great mom," said John, turning his hose toward the rosebushes.

But her husband couldn't handle being a father and moved out when Jeremiah was two or three, John couldn't remember. He did remember watching her struggle to balance a full-time job with single parenthood. But she did it, thanks to her own grit, and also to an elderly woman in the neighborhood who ran a small day-care center in her house.

As a boy, Jeremiah seemed close to his mom. Anne went to all his Little League games in the spring and summer, drove Jeremiah and his friends to the movies, and even served as a den mother for the local Cub Scout pack. John described Jeremiah as a "sweet kid," a phrase that Mark suspected he didn't use much.

When he was thirteen, Jeremiah was struck and killed by a car. Three years ago, he, Brad, and two other friends were crossing a busy highway on the way home from a movie they didn't have permission to see and to which Anne had refused to drive them. He survived only a few hours in a local hospital before dying.

When John reached that part of the story, he turned his face toward the rosebushes and said, "It was a tough time for my son." He bit his lip and continued with the rest of the story: the crying they heard from Anne's house that night and the next day, the funeral on a humid Memorial Day weekend with Jeremiah's friends serving as honorary pallbearers, the flower baskets that crowded her front step for days until they wilted under the sun. Anne shut herself inside the house for the next few weeks.

John swept the rosebushes with a bath of water. Mark felt a faint cool mist on his face.

It was difficult for Mark to take it all in. All he had asked was, "So what's my landlady's story?"

Such a strange thing to hear on a warm evening just before sunset with the fireflies winking on and off. So much sadness unearthed in a few minutes. Mark remembered the conversation with Brad's father now, as Anne sat beside him in his truck.

Anne looked out the window as Mark drove on. "I hate that car."

"You know," Mark said to change the topic and to cheer himself up, "I don't even know what you do. I've known you for a year, and I'm not sure what you do."

"That's funny." She turned and faced him with a sly smile. "What do you *think* I do?"

Mark grimaced. In college one of his girlfriends asked with depressing regularity, "Guess what I'd like to do tonight?" and he always seemed to give the wrong answer. Usually his girlfriend wanted to either go out to dinner or see a movie; he wanted to stay home and have sex. Once, despairing of answering correctly, he opted to say what he really wanted: "Polish off a six-pack, watch the Celtics, make love, and go to sleep." She sulked for the rest of the night.

He tried to imagine what Anne did. All he could think of was the sight of her in those gray yoga pants. "A yoga instructor?"

Anne laughed loudly, the first genuine laughter he'd ever heard from her. She had a sexy laugh, deeper than he expected.

"Thanks," she said, shaking her head and looking out the window. "I'll have to tell everyone in my yoga class that. No, nothing that interesting. I'm just an accountant."

"Really?"

"Why?" she said turning toward him again. "You don't think I'm smart enough? That I'm some sort of soccer . . ." She paused before she got to the word "mom."

"No, no," Mark said, trying to fend off any mention of her son. "It's just that I always see you in the yoga outfit and you seem too, um, mellow to be an accountant."

She smiled, pleased by the small compliment, and tapped the dashboard absentmindedly. "Yeah, that's me—mellow CPA. You should talk to people in the office. I think they wish I *were* mellow."

They drove together in silence, windows down, enjoying the evening air, which suddenly had grown cooler. He looked through his windshield at the heavy clouds. It was definitely going to rain.

"Shit!" he shouted, just as they were turning onto the Blue Route.

"What's the matter?"

"I left my cell phone at the abbey."

She sighed and pursed her lips, anxious to get home and uninterested in going to the abbey.

"Do you mind if we stop by there?" he said. "I can't live without my phone."

"You're doing *me* the favor, remember?" she said. "Stop by, and I'll wait in the car."

6

B y the time they reached the Abbey of Saints Philip
and James, rain was drumming loudly on the roof
of the truck. Anne hadn't set foot on the monastery
grounds since she was a girl, but when Mark pulled onto the
driveway, she remembered it all: the vast green lawns and
endless meadows where she used to hunt for grasshoppers
and crickets, the tall pine trees that lined the driveway like
sentinels, and the way the church steeple slowly rose over the
driveway as you approached it. "Like a ship's mast coming
over the horizon," she suddenly remembered her dad saying.
She was amazed that she recalled that phrase. Where did that
come from?

Both her parents were religious—her father extremely, her
mother fairly. An accountant like Anne, her father helped
the monks with their books, mainly during tax season. As
far as she could recall, he was on a parish retreat when he
met Father Edward, the monk with the bad breath, and they
had remained friends. But she was vague about that. Once
or twice he brought Anne to the monastery, and she remem-

bered it as a not unpleasant place, but not pleasant either. Sometimes she'd sit on a bench in some hallway outside the chapel when the monks were singing, but most of the time she sat in an office, doodling with colored pencils on plain sheets of typing paper while her father worked on the books and monks dropped by to chat. For a silent monastery, they certainly talked a lot. She recalled being inside the chapel once.

Or maybe not. Maybe that was some other church. She had long ago given up on going to church, except for weddings and funerals.

What she remembered most about the abbey was its smell. It was incense of course, but a special kind she hadn't smelled before or since. It was quite unlike the incense she smelled whenever she passed that Zen bookstore she liked in Philly, where the slender sticks of sandalwood burning outside the entrance produced an acrid smell. The monastery's scent was different. Sweeter somehow. At least in her memory.

"We'll go in the back way," said Mark. He drove up the driveway, turned left onto a blacktopped road, splashed loudly through a shallow puddle, and passed a sign that said, "Enclosure. No Entrance Please."

Not only do the monks live on a huge piece of property in a wealthy suburb, thought Anne, *but they put up signs to make people feel unwelcome. Seems unchristian.*

Mark pulled into a parking lot outside a modest wooden building with a red-and-white plaque over the door that read, "Monastery Jams."

"*That's* where they make the jam?" she said. "It looks tiny."

"Things look different from the inside. It's bigger than it seems. Why don't you come in for a bit?" he said over the rain, which was letting up. "I can get you a cup of coffee. And they have some amazing coffee in the retreat wing."

"No, thanks. I'm fine here."

"Oh come *on*. They're not going to bite."

She exhaled. "Okay."

They emerged from the car, tried unsuccessfully to dodge the raindrops, sprinted around the side of the jam building, and walked quickly up a flagstone path. She didn't remember this part of the monastery. It was lovely. Even in the light rain, with her head down, Anne was aware of the lush grass, the carefully pruned pine trees, the well-tended azaleas, the full rhododendron bushes.

"Oh God," she said sharply. "What's *this*?"

"Oh," he said, suddenly flustered. "The cemetery."

She could see that the monks were buried here with a minimum of fuss, laid to rest in a small plot that held perhaps fifty of them, with white metal crosses, only a foot or so tall, marking the spots. She glanced at Mark and noticed his discomfort at having brought her this way.

"It's fine," she said. "Let's just go out another way when we leave, okay?"

The flagstone path led to an archway with a door. Mark opened it for her.

7

Central air for this big building? Anne thought as she stepped inside the cool of the monastery. *No wonder they have to sell so much jam.*

Then the aroma hit her. She hadn't experienced it for years, and instantly it called up a precise memory from childhood: her reaching up to hold her father's hand as she walked through the monastery. Something like flowers but not flowers, something like perfume but not perfume, something like a fire in a fireplace, but not that either. The overpowering scent made her want to pause and think about her father.

Anne remembered her Psych 101 professor at Haverford saying that smell was the most primal of senses, tapping directly into our brains. This, she knew, was what was happening. But it moved her nonetheless. She wanted to tell someone how much she missed her father and how much she wished she could talk with him about Jeremiah. But she didn't know Mark well at all. So she just inhaled. *If I could smell this every day, I might be happier.*

Mark led her down a long hallway whose plain brick walls were lined with silky white robes hanging on wooden pegs.

"What are those?" she asked.

"Sorry," he whispered. "We can't talk that loudly. They like to keep things quiet here."

That was something she disliked about church: people were always telling you what not to do.

"Fine," she said in a loud whisper. "What are *those*?" She pointed to the robes.

"Cowls. The monks use them during their prayers, which are going to start soon. It's almost time for Vespers. Wanna go to Vespers while I'm looking for my phone?"

"No thanks."

"It's pretty impressive," he said enthusiastically. "You might enjoy it."

"No," she said firmly, "that's okay."

"Okeydoke." He invited her to sit on a long wooden bench in the hall, while he began his search for his cell phone.

"I think I know where to find it," he said, walking off into the darkness.

It was certainly dark. *Maybe they should spend less money on air conditioning and more on lightbulbs,* she thought. The hallways were dim, at least the one in which she now sat. An ornate wooden cabinet, made of the darkest pine, stood against an opposite wall. Its drawers, which bore carvings of flowers and leaves and the heads of chubby little angels, were tightly shut, and its gleaming polished top was bare. *If*

*that were in my home, it would be piled high with letters and books
and magazines.*

With her back resting comfortably against cool brown
bricks, Anne was suddenly aware of her fatigue.

She sat in one end of a series of four hallways that formed a
perfect square and enclosed a large glassed-in garden. In the
center of the garden was a white marble fountain, the size of
a birdbath, surrounded by four large ornamental cherry trees
in full bloom. In the rain their wrinkled trunks were a shiny
black and their blossoms glossy pink. Azaleas glowed in red
profusion. Either the monks were talented gardeners, or they
had hired some good landscapers, because she had never seen
such a well-tended plot, lush with grass and carefully nurtured
trees and bushes.

Something about the view seemed familiar, but she couldn't
remember if she had seen the garden when she was little or
even if she had been to this part of the abbey. It didn't register
the way the steeple and the incense had. Anne stared at the
garden as if she were seeing something she knew in a deep
way while not being sure. As if she both remembered it and
was seeing it for the first time. The feeling unsettled her.

A tall, thin monk appeared, wearing long white-and-black
robes. She remembered their outfits well enough: Father
Edward dressed like that. Sometimes he had food on his
robes too. As the monk silently glided past her, he nodded and
smiled, pulled a cowl from one of the pegs on the wall, swiftly
tossed it over his habit, expertly arranged the hood so that it

fell back neatly over his shoulders, and slipped into a doorway to her right.

A loud bell tolled, startling her. She instinctively looked up and realized that the bell must be in the steeple outside. It rang out single notes, then more insistently, with the tones coming every few seconds.

Within moments, several monks materialized, emerging from doorways she hadn't noticed. Single file, they walked down opposite sides of the hallway, some looking at the glassed-in garden, some with eyes fixed on the dark red tile floor, nearly all with hands hidden within the folds of their habits. Some were ancient and used wooden canes and metal walkers, moving deliberately. Two were surprisingly young, perhaps in their late twenties, though it was hard to tell with their downturned faces and close-cropped hair. Most were late-middle-aged men who gave the impression of having made this walk many times. Only a few glanced at her as they passed. She figured there were about twenty-five monks in all.

One man, pale, tall, with thinning hair, a receding chin, and Buddy Holly glasses, smiled as he approached, slowed his pace, and bent over to address her. He had watery blue eyes. Anne was surprised to feel a desire to know him.

"Welcome," he whispered. "Can I help you?"

"I'm with Mark Matthews," she said. "He's lost . . . I mean, he lost his cell phone, and I'm waiting for him. Am I in the wrong place?"

Another tall monk, with close-cropped sandy hair, stopped and paused before her bench. "Are you Anne?"

How the hell does he know my name? she wondered.

Seeing her confusion, he whispered, "I'm Brother Robert. Mark told me he was going to pick you up tonight."

Mark talks about me here?

The monk with the big glasses asked, "Would you like to join us for Vespers? I can take you to the visitors' section, if you'd like."

"No, thank you," she said politely. "I'm fine here."

"Okay," he said. "We'll pray for you."

Anne never knew how to respond to that. Well-meaning friends often said it after Jeremiah's death. She wasn't sure if she still believed in God, so she thought it was hypocritical to say thanks, as if she *wanted* them to pray to God. And what would she tell them if nothing happened? If she didn't feel any better? They'd probably be disappointed that their prayers hadn't worked, and the last thing she needed was more disappointment in the air. So usually she just said, "Okay." Which was what she said now to the monk with the Buddy Holly glasses.

He smiled at her again and walked into the chapel behind the other monk.

Why was Mark talking about me to the monks? So rude.

She leaned against the cold brick wall and closed her eyes. She could rest while the monks did their prayers. How tired she always felt.

Then she heard the first note of the organ, a low tone that seemed to make her heart vibrate.

A strong baritone voice echoed from the church, singing,

"Let my evening prayer ascend before you, O Lord . . ."

Then the rest of the monks answered, chanting, "And may your loving-kindness descend upon us."

Instinctively, she looked around to see if anyone else was in the hallways listening. But she was alone. The monks chanted their prayers with growing confidence. Were they singing psalms? She wasn't sure. And were the psalms in the Old Testament or the New Testament? She wasn't sure about that either. Though she wasn't a believer, she decided that as long as she was here, she might as well enjoy the beautiful music. She had occasionally wondered what "Vespers" meant and imagined it as a boring prayer service with lots of Bible readings and dull sermons. But this was lovely.

After a few psalms and a reading that she couldn't quite hear, the monks began to sing something that sounded like a real song, a hymn. The first few notes tugged at her memory.

Yes! How could she have forgotten? Anne's father hummed that tune when he was working around the house. That's right. Her mom used to tease him about it. "Oh, honeybunch, please. Not that *hymn* again. Pretty soon you'll be making jam!"

Her father's hymn. She closed her eyes and allowed the song to carry her to her past. Sleepy now, she started to nod off. Then she had an image of her father holding Jeremiah after his birth, in the hospital, and she felt the hollow in her stomach open up. The memory of how much her father loved his grandson was like a knife in her heart. *Jeremiah, I miss you so much!*

Her normal defenses weakened by drowsiness, Anne began to cry. She couldn't help it. She was so tired—and it felt as if the incense and music were touching her innermost parts. On some days she thought that sadness would overwhelm her, drown her, destroy her.

Reaching into her backpack for a Kleenex, she heard the bell toll. The monks began to file out of the chapel. She wiped her eyes. Just what she didn't need: to be caught crying in the hallway.

The monk with the Buddy Holly glasses was standing over her. "Are you okay?"

Anne was determined not to look foolish. "Yes, I'm fine," she said, and shook her head up and down quickly. "I'm just fine." But she started crying again, though she was trying hard to stop. The tears that she didn't want came anyway.

When the monk sat next to her, she worried that he would put his arm around her, but he didn't. He just sat there, as the other monks silently passed and disappeared into the doorways from which they had materialized. Anne wiped her eyes. She shifted slightly, and the wooden bench creaked loudly. After a while she spoke.

"My son died."

"I'm so sorry," said the monk. "May he rest in peace."

She nodded and paused. "Thank you."

"When did he die, if I may ask?"

"Three years ago." She thought it sounded absurd. The monk would think that she should be over her grief by now. He wouldn't say it, but he would *think* it.

"Very recently then," he said. Anne looked at him with a mixture of gratitude and surprise.

"Yes," she said. "That's right."

"Oh, I'm so sorry. What was his name?"

Anne noticed that he wasn't whispering. She began to sob. Saying her son's name sometimes made her cry, as if she were summoning his memory in a more concrete way, making him present to herself and others. But she couldn't believe she was crying in front of someone she didn't know.

"I'm so embarrassed," she said. "This is so embarrassing."

The monk looked down at his black-and-white habit and waited.

"Jeremiah," she said, finally.

They both noticed Mark approaching.

"I found it!" said Mark, in a loud whisper, holding his cell phone over his head as he loped across the red tiles. Anne withdrew from the monk, dried her tears, and shoved the Kleenex pack into her backpack.

8

Mark saw her tears and seemed unnerved by them. "I see you've met the abbot," he said.

"You're the abbot?" said Anne, turning to the monk.

"I'm sorry," said the monk, who stood, as if formality were now in order. "I didn't even introduce myself. I'm Father Paul." He offered his hand, and she shook it.

"He's the *abbot*," said Mark.

"Yes, I got that," Anne said, looking perturbed. She stood up and then said to Paul, "Nice to meet you."

"Where was the phone?" asked Paul.

"Oh," said Mark. "I'm an idiot. I looked all over for it, but then I found it in chapel. I guess I left it there when I was changing the flowers from last week."

"Did you pray to St. Anthony?"

Mark looked at him blankly.

"Oh, come on," said Anne. "Even I know that one: 'St. Anthony, St. Anthony please come around. Something is lost and cannot be found.'"

"Oh, a Catholic!" said Paul.

"Sort of," she said.

"I see. Are you from around here?"

"Oh yeah, a Philly girl. All my life."

"Have you been to the abbey before?"

"Funny enough," she said, "my father used to bring me here when I was little. Believe it or not, he used to do the books here. He was friends with one of the monks—a Father Edward, I think. In fact, I'm pretty sure that he baptized me."

Father Paul smiled. "Oh yes, Father Edward sometimes got special permission to do baptisms for the children of people who worked here. He's quite old now of course, but he still—"

"He's still *alive*? He must be a hundred years old!"

Paul laughed. "Oh no, Father Edward's only about eighty. But I guess he must have seemed old to you when you were little. Would you like to visit him? He's in our infirmary at the moment. I'm sure he'd love to see what happened to the baby he baptized."

Anne was alarmed by the sudden invitation. "No thanks." She hoped the abbot couldn't tell that this was the last thing she'd like to do right now. Then, feeling guilty, she said, "But tell him I said hi. And tell him that my father liked him a lot." That was true. Her father used to love telling Anne's mom funny stories that Father Edward told him about the other monks. His favorite was about the addled monk who tried to wash his clothes in the dishwasher.

"I'll tell him tonight that I met you," said Paul. "He'll be happy to hear it. And happy that you stopped by to visit us."

Anne thought that was a generous thing to say. The abbot made sitting on a bench for a few minutes sound like some big act of charity.

"Well," said Mark, "we should get going."

A gust of wind swept through the cloister garden, shaking branches on the trees, and the rain started again. In a few seconds it became a downpour.

"You know what?" said Mark. "Let me pull the truck around to the front of the church, so we won't have to walk down that path in this rain. Is that okay, Father Paul?" Anne was relieved they would be able to avoid the cemetery.

Paul nodded, and Mark darted out a door. "Woo-hoo!" he shouted cheerfully as he ran through the rain. Paul grinned as he watched Mark skitter down the flagstone path, momentarily lose his balance on the slippery gray stones, right himself, and jump into his truck.

"That Mark," said Paul. "He amazes us with his energy. He's a holy man, you know, in his own way."

Anne had absolutely no clue how to respond to that, so she just nodded.

Once Mark was in his truck, Paul turned to Anne and said, "As Jesus said, 'Follow me.'"

"Are you allowed to say things like that?" asked Anne as they walked over the tiled floors.

"I just did," said Paul with a wide, gap-toothed grin. "Besides, who's going to correct me? I'm the abbot."

When they entered the chapel, Paul knelt on his right knee and quickly stood up. Anne did too, out of courtesy.

The chapel had a high dark-timbered ceiling, a red tile floor identical to the hallway floor, and stained-glass windows with chunky blue and white glass arranged in abstract designs. The altar was a colossal block of gray stone, impossibly heavy. Anne wondered how on earth the monks brought it into the chapel. Draped on the altar was a long white cloth, apparently recently ironed: there was not a wrinkle on it. Its hemmed ends lightly brushed the floor. Two twisty wrought-iron candlesticks sat on either end of the altar, each holding a fat white candle.

Hovering above the altar, supported by nearly invisible wires, was a peculiar crucifix. The cross itself was simple: plain wood painted red. Jesus's body was made of black metal, and his nailed hands were not raised over his head, as in other crucifixes Anne had seen, but perpendicular to his body. And his head did not loll; rather, his face, sad and severe, looked straight out, which disturbed her.

Overall, though, it looked like most large 1950s Catholic churches. Except for one prominent architectural feature. Occupying the front half of the church, where you would expect to find pews facing the altar, were two consecutive rows of wooden stalls, which faced each another, on opposite sides of the church. Each set of stalls, in blond wood, had approximately forty seats. Anne tried to puzzle out the purpose of this arrangement.

"This is where the monks sit while we pray," said Paul as they passed through the middle. "Some sit on one side, and some on the other. That way we can see one another. It helps us feel more like a community when we're together."

Centered on one side wall of the church was a framed portrait of the Virgin Mary painted on a white canvas. Supported by an iron stand, it stood on a heavy wooden table with elaborately carved legs. Beside it was a flimsy metal table upon which a thin, fluted glass vase stuffed with red roses was placed.

Wearing a dark red dress, an olive-skinned Mary held in her arms Jesus, who was clad in a white robe. Jesus's mother seemed to be looking directly at Anne. Her expression was inscrutable—a mixture of sadness, resignation, and defiance. Anne suddenly found herself wondering whether Mary ever knew what would happen to her son. Did she have a clue? Anne had never thought of that before. Was that in the Bible? Did Mary know that her little boy would end up being killed? Did anything prepare her for what was to come?

Father Paul was busy ticking off the times of day that the monks prayed, but Anne wasn't paying attention. For a few seconds, as Father Paul talked, she focused on the portrait, which met her gaze and held it, as if to say, "I know."

"Let's go this way," said Paul, and he led her past the monks' stalls, down the main aisle, and past a waist-high brick wall with an opening in its center. On this side of the wall were standard pews, highly polished, which faced the front of the church, in the style Anne was accustomed to.

"Our visitors sit in this part of the church," he said. *Why didn't the visitors pray with the monks?* she wondered.

When Paul opened the front door, a wet breeze swept through the church. Some leaves skittered into the church, and Paul pushed them back outside with his sandaled foot. The two stepped onto the portico and saw Mark's truck in the front of the parking lot, the door open for her.

"Would you mind waiting a second?" asked Paul, who ducked into the church.

Mark rolled down the window of his truck. "Where's Father Paul going?"

Anne shrugged.

Paul emerged from the church. "I saw you admiring our icon," he said, pressing a small card into her hand, "and I thought you might like this."

Anne looked at the image of Mary and Jesus. A few heavy drops fell from the eaves onto the card. Something was written on the back.

"Thanks," she said, touched by the small kindness.

"Come back anytime," said Paul. "You're always welcome. And maybe you could visit with Father Edward. I'm sure he'd love that."

"Thanks," she said, though she had no intention of seeing the old priest with bad breath.

Anne dashed a few feet in the rain and climbed into the truck. As Mark pulled out of the parking lot, she admired the tall pine trees that lined the driveway, whose heavy boughs dripped rainwater onto the grass.

"He's nice, isn't he?" said Mark. "Father Paul's a nice guy."

"Yes," she said, staring out the window. "Seems so."

She shoved the card into her pocket and felt it wetly bend.

9

By the time Mark pulled into her driveway, the rain had passed, leaving the air fresher. Anne was grateful for the ride. It was generous of Mark, though she wondered whether that's what made someone "holy," as Father Paul said. Was Mark some sort of saint? He didn't seem like one. For one thing, he partied too much and dated a seemingly endless parade of women. At least that's what Brad's father told her. She doubted that saints did that.

Anne checked her mailbox, opened the door, pushed back her dog, and threw her keys on the round kitchen table. Then she set out some dog food in Sunshine's dented metal bowl and sat down to the sound of his contented chewing. Though there were four chairs around the table, Anne sat where she had when Jeremiah and Eddie were still with her, in the seat nearest the sink. She had never once sat in Jeremiah's seat after his death. It was his place.

She unbound the packet of mail, which the mailman had helpfully bound with a thick rubber band. Bills and ads, mainly. *Entertainment Weekly,* a guilty pleasure. *The New Yorker,* for the fiction, not the cartoons. *The Economist,* which she got hooked on in college, even though she was the only person she knew who read it. And a card from her cousin. She slit it open with a steak knife, grudgingly. Elizabeth had a way with cards, and Anne was unsurprised to see a yellow sun holding hands with another yellow sun. Both suns were smiling. "Love!" said a little word balloon coming from the mouths of both suns.

"Oh *God,*" said Anne out loud.

On the inside her cousin had written, "I know Jeremiah's birthday is coming up, and I wanted you to know that I was thinking of you. Lots of love, Elizabeth. OXOXOX."

One of the happiest days in her life had become a day that depressed her. The only day she dreaded more was the anniversary of his death. She stared at the suns and hated their stupid happy faces. One day she would tell her cousin that if she was going to send a card that mentions someone's dead child, she should make sure it doesn't have anyone, much less any celestial objects, grinning.

As she settled into the chair, Anne felt something shift in her pants pocket; she pulled out the card from the monastery. It was slightly wrinkled where the rainwater had touched it.

Mary's face hadn't looked so sad in the abbey. On the card, however, she seemed on the verge of tears. Or maybe she was just serious. It was strange seeing a picture of a mother holding her baby and looking somber.

Anne's father used to pray the Rosary every night, and her mother kept a blue-and-white porcelain statue of Mary on her nightstand, but otherwise Anne didn't know very much about Jesus's mother. Sometimes she wished she knew more about the Bible. All she remembered from Sunday school were drawing pictures of Noah's ark, singing Christmas carols, and fashioning clay models of Jesus's tomb. She thought again about Mary.

Would Mary have given birth to Jesus if she knew what was going to happen to him? Of course he did rise from the dead, but how could she stand to see him suffer? Anne once saw a movie in which Mary knelt at the bottom of the cross while Jesus was being crucified, then gripped the cross, and screamed.

Mary had a son, she thought suddenly. Anne didn't know why she had never thought of it like that before. She felt stupid. Mary was Jesus's mother, of course. But somehow when she thought of the words, "Mary had a son," it sounded different. Felt different. And Mary had a son who died. Did someone have to tell her when her son was going to be crucified? Did they have to run through Jerusalem to find her on Good Friday? Did someone have to say "Mary, come quickly! They're doing it." Whose terrible job was it to tell Mary?

Anne remembered opening the door and seeing the police on her doorstep, on that summer night.

She turned the card over.

At the cross her station keeping,
Stood the mournful Mother weeping,
Close to Jesus to the last.
O Mary, Mother of Sorrows, pray for us!

When she read the words about being close to Jesus, her throat tightened. That's exactly how she felt when she saw Jeremiah in the hospital bed. She wasn't embarrassed that she screamed when the police told her the news. She wasn't embarrassed that she couldn't stop crying in the police car on the way to the hospital, the sirens tearing apart the humid night air. She wasn't embarrassed that people heard her wail when she first saw him in the intensive-care unit. She just wanted to be near Jeremiah. His hair looked the way it did when he had a fever—damp, plastered to his head. But now it was caked in blood. She knew when she saw him that he was dying. Because somehow Jeremiah didn't look like Jeremiah.

All she wanted to do was to be close to him. She wanted to hold him so tight that he would never leave her.

Anne stared at the words on the back of the card. "Close to Jesus to the last." She placed her hand over her mouth and sobbed. She hated the monk for giving her this card, and she was grateful to him. Sunshine nuzzled her ankles.

"It's okay," she said to the dog and petted its golden brown head.

Carefully, Anne dried the card with a paper towel and affixed it to her refrigerator door with a red Phillies magnet Jeremiah bought for her the first time he went to a game.

IO

The abbot could hardly believe how much work he had to do that night.

One of the things that occasionally bothered Father Paul about being abbot was what "seculars," those outside the monastery, would say about his work. "It must be nice not to have any responsibilities," said one wealthy Catholic benefactor who paid him a visit a few days ago. He set aside his annoyance, because the monastery depended on her generous benefactions.

"Well," he said, "It's *ora et labora*. Prayer *and* work. I'm actually quite busy."

"Oh, I'm sure," she said airily, though he could tell she didn't believe him.

When Paul entered the novitiate, his friends had one of two reactions. They thought either that Paul was wasting his life, after having finished his Ph.D. in church history and then securing a tenure-track position at Villanova, or that he was entering a perfect world where strife was unknown, mortal problems were banished, and a rich prayer life was the norm.

Neither was accurate. Paul knew his vocation wasn't a waste of a life; it was a fulfillment of it. A few years after he entered, he was asked by the abbot to teach church history to the novices. "We'll use all your talents here," said the abbot. "God gave them to you, and then God gave you to us." And he enjoyed putting his skills to use. Later, after he was appointed novice director, Paul sent a postcard with a picture of the abbey to his former department chair at Villanova. "Teaching again," he wrote. "And no committees!" The department head wrote back on a postcard, saying, "Sign me up."

As for the monastic life being without strife, Paul often told the story of Brother Francis, a monk, now long dead, who had a unique way of communicating his displeasure with his fellow monks. Whenever the monks chanted a psalm that mentioned the word "enemy"—as in "Rescue me from my enemies, O God"—Brother Francis would pointedly look up from his prayer book and glare at whichever monk was annoying him that week.

And a consistently rich prayer life? Paul had been a monk long enough to know that the spiritual life was one of ups and downs. Often he felt close to God—in his private prayer, while praying in community, or during the busyness of the day. Sometimes a word or phrase from the psalms seemed to pierce his heart like an arrow. Many times a Gospel story he had heard dozens of times over the years seemed brand new, as if he had never heard it before, taking on an irresistible urgency. Just as often, he would be laughing with a fellow monk about some craziness in the abbey and feel a burst of consolation about his life. And a few times Paul had what he later realized were truly mystical experiences. Once, during Vespers, he felt utterly filled with God's expansive love, as if his heart were not big enough to contain it. He treasured all these moments.

But he also knew that the spiritual life had its dry patches— sometimes long dry patches—when God didn't feel close at all. Prayer could seem routine, even boring. *If I have to sing this psalm one more time,* he once caught himself thinking, *my head is going to explode.* Mass could be, he had to admit, dull at times. And his personal prayer was sometimes filled with distractions. Oddly, though, the longer he was a monk and the more he read the writings of the great spiritual masters (all of whom experienced more or less the same thing), the less he worried about dry periods. It was like any relationship: things couldn't be exciting all the time. *Perhaps,* Paul thought a few years back, *the human heart couldn't take it, if God were always so close.*

Life in the monastery was fulfilling. It was also busy. For his sister he had once typed up the schedule of an abbot's typical day—"The Abbatial Day"—along with the names of the various times of prayer. Paul loved the word "abbatial." It was absurdly pretentious, so he used it as often as he could to get a laugh from the other monks. "Please sit on the abbatial couch, Father."

Paul kept that page, which he copied and sent to friends on the outside, since they so often asked, "What does an abbot do all day?" He wished he had it on hand when that benefactor made her comment.

The Abbatial Day

3:30 A.M.: Vigils. The first prayer of the day, and my favorite. It took me almost a year to get used to the schedule, but after that I found that I loved praying in the dark, before the day has begun.

4:15–6:00: Breakfast. A simple meal, followed by some quiet prayer and spiritual reading in my room (my "cell," as we call it), and of course showering, shaving, and so on.

6:00: Lauds. Daily Mass follows. I'm usually the celebrant for the major feasts, but I take my turn with the other priests here for the rest of the Masses.

7:00: Spiritual reading, correspondence, preparing talks for the monks in "chapter," our community meetings. This is when I write my homilies too, if it's my turn to preside the next day.

9:00–12:00: Visiting the monks in the infirmary; checking in at the jam factory; meeting with the "cellarer," the monk in charge of food and provisions; and speaking with the director of the physical plant about the grounds and such. This is when I sometimes feel like I'm running a small town.

10:00: Terce. This prayer can be said wherever I am, for example, in the jam factory.

12:15 P.M.: Sext. At this point in the day, I can find myself nodding off during our prayer—not a good thing for the abbot to do.

12:30: Dinner. The food's quite good. And since I'm the abbot, I can make sure of that!

1:00: Cleaning up in the kitchen.

2:00: None. This prayer is so named because it is in the "ninth hour" of the day after dawn. (It's pronounced "known," by the way.)

2:15–5:30: Spiritual reading, more correspondence and e-mail, chapter talks, checking on the sick monks in the infirmary, visiting the working monks, meeting with monks who run other parts of the monastery, with a break for personal prayer.

5:30: Vespers.

6:00–7:30: Supper, cleaning up, private meetings with the monks or spiritual direction. This is when I sometimes see people "on the outside."

7:30: Compline. The last prayer of the day. At the end of Compline I bless all the monks with holy water before we retire for bed. To see the older monks, some of whom trained me, bow their heads and ask for a blessing is humbling.

8:00: Leisure reading, catching up on the papers, bedtime. I'm usually beat.

Being abbot was something Paul never aspired to. Nor could he have imagined he'd be a candidate. But as the election approached three years ago, he began to sense that the monks were looking for a younger man to take over. As a

middle-aged monk who had completed his formation, spent
time as the novice director, and was in decent health (except
for a persistently bad back), he suspected that he would probably be in the running. But it turned out that Paul's election
was a surprise only to him. He won on the first ballot.

Even with his responsibilities, and even though he missed
the simpler life of a monk, life as an abbot suited him. Paul
seemed to be good at it, and in general the monks liked him.
Most of them. There were always people in the community
who didn't get along, and didn't get along with him. One
monk, who disliked Paul from the day he entered the novitiate, turned red when Paul was elected. So Paul tried to treat
him with extra care. But he liked being abbot. And he loved
living here.

On the other hand, as he often reminded seculars, life at
the Abbey of Saints Philip and James was not perfect. Despite their best intentions, monks argued, grew angry at one
another, and occasionally held grudges. Monks were still imperfect, and sinful. As Paul knew he was. A line from Thomas
Merton, the Trappist monk whose books he had first read in
high school, put things in perspective: "The first and most elementary test of one's call to the religious life—whether as
a Jesuit, Franciscan, Cistercian, or Carthusian—is the willing-
ness to accept life in a community in which everybody is more
or less imperfect." Paul memorized the line and often used it
with the novices.

John Berchmans, a Jesuit saint he read about in the novitiate, wrote, *Vita communis est mea maxima penitentia.* Some

pious scholars translated *vita communis* as the "common life," that is, the everyday life of men and women—getting up, going to work, struggling through life, and so on. But Paul suspected another meaning was more likely. "Life in community," life in a religious order, was his greatest penance. On cold winter days when a third of the monks had the flu, a third were sullen, and another third were angry at him for some decision he had made, Paul prayed to St. John Berchmans.

Paul often thought that he might amend Berchmans's quote to read, "Life in community is my greatest penance and greatest blessing." He loved so many things—from the first day he entered. During his first week at the monastery he told his novice master that he loved it so much that he wanted to sing. Father Edward responded, "Well, then it's a good thing we do sing—several times a day!"

His other loves were easy to name. Paul loved the structured schedule, which freed him from wondering how to arrange his day. He was also happy not to worry about where he would be in the future. His brothers and sisters seemed to move from job to job every few years, and last year one brother had to relocate his family from Philadelphia to North Carolina. By contrast, Paul was planted here until he died, when he would be buried in the cemetery. "Here's my future home," he once said to his sister, when they passed by the rows of white crosses. She found it morbid. He found it comforting. At the end of his novitiate, Paul took the monastic vows of obedience, conversion of life (in other words, to live like a monk), and stability. Stability was the easiest vow for him.

He loved praying—singing really—in common with his brother monks, because when he was happy about his vocation and wanted to shout to God, he could do so; and when he was doubting his vocation, there were others who were not and who could carry him along with their prayers.

Seeing the seasons change on this magnificent plot of land was another joy for Paul. On stormy days Paul could peer out the window of the dormitory to watch the tall green pine trees bend in the wind, and that was beautiful. On snowy days he could watch the roof of the jam factory pile with wet snow, and that was beautiful. And on spring days, his favorite, he could admire the cherry and dogwood trees in the cloister garden that burst into pink and white flower, and that was the most beautiful of all.

The abbot stared out the window at the violet sky, then sat down at his desk, took out a note card with a photo of the cloister garden, and started to write a note to a woman who had just donated a stack of Bible commentaries. Not only did the library already have that particular series of books, but they were old and out of date. Paul wanted to thank her anyway.

II

For the next few days, Anne couldn't get that line out of her mind: "Close to Jesus to the last." That's exactly how she felt with Jeremiah. On the ride to work the next Friday, she kept her radio off, so that she could try to figure out why these words hit home. As she passed the exit for the monastery, she momentarily considered stopping at the chapel to see the picture of Mary again, and then laughed.

"Oh, I'm sure *that* would go over well!" she said aloud in the car. She shook her head, imagining the reaction when she told her boss that she was late to work because she was visiting a monastery.

After Jeremiah's death, Anne was grateful that she had a job. Of course there was no question that she would continue working; even with the rent from the second house, she had to support herself. But after the accident and the wake and the funeral and the weeks inside the house, she was, finally, relieved to have something to take her mind off her grief. After a few months she started to feel trapped by the house, as if it were crushing her with memories. So even though she found it nearly impossible to concentrate and everyone treated her as if she were a fragile glass vase, she eventually called her boss and told him she was coming back, and she was happy that she did.

Those lines about Mary stayed with her. During her lunch break that Friday, she went online, found a search engine, and typed in the words "Close to Jesus to the last."

Lots of super-Catholic images popped up on her screen, the kind of stuff she loathed. A kitschy picture of a lily-white Mary holding a bloody, dead Jesus. A Flemish painting of the Crucifixion, with a weeping Mary and another person standing at the foot of the cross. And a painting from Jesus's point of view from the cross, with Mary and some other women collapsed in sorrow as the Roman soldiers looked on. In a few clicks she discovered that the quote was taken from a lengthy prayer called the Stabat Mater, about Mary standing by the cross. Anne started to read the prayer, but lost interest. She didn't like the rest of the prayer, just the lines on her card. Again, Jeremiah came into her mind and heart.

Suddenly, she was angry with herself. *What am I doing looking at all this religious stuff? What bullshit.* God hadn't helped her when Jeremiah was dying. God certainly hadn't helped Jeremiah. God wasn't close to her, or Jeremiah, or anyone.

She clicked off the page, popped her head into the office next door, and asked her younger colleague, Kerry, if she wanted to get a bite for lunch.

"Sure," said Kerry. "What are you up to?"

"Nothing," said Anne. "Wasting time on the web."

By the end of the day, she felt an unfamiliar mix of emotions. Jeremiah was on her mind, as always. After three years, she was getting used to that, and used to feeling that her insides would open up whenever she thought about him. The therapist she saw for a few months after Jeremiah's death told her that thinking of him so frequently was normal. But now there was something else: curiosity about the monastery, especially about that painting.

12

On her way home, Anne approached the exit to the abbey on the Blue Route. She grew increasingly annoyed with herself, wondering why she kept thinking about that painting of Mary. It seemed a waste of time. How could she ever know what Mary felt anyway?

She was also wondering about putting her grief behind her. Or if she ever could. As was often the case, Anne was confused not only about what she was feeling, but about what she was *supposed* to be feeling. What was normal? She didn't want to forget Jeremiah—that would be impossible—but she wished that she could stop obsessing over his death, stop turning it over and over in her mind. She wanted to remember him only as alive, not dead. Was that even possible? The therapist had told her that whatever she felt was normal. "Let yourself feel what you feel," she had said. "There's no timetable for grief."

The image of Mary returned to her thoughts again, insistently.

Mary didn't have to grieve much over Jesus—just three

days, right? Then he was back. Jeremiah had been dead for three *years*.

"Try that, Mary," she said in the car, out loud. Then she felt guilty about saying it. But she didn't know if she believed in God anyway, so who cared?

So she said it again, "Try that, Mary." She felt better telling Mary, and maybe God, exactly what she felt.

Then she felt ashamed. Mary had watched her son suffer for three hours on the cross. Anne remembered holding Jeremiah's hand in his hospital bed for three hours, until his death. She held him tight even after the doctors told her that he was "gone." Gone. What a stupid thing to say. Gone where?

Mary would understand her holding on. One mother would understand another. Anne felt her throat tighten; she wanted to speak to another woman who had lost a child. What would Mary say?

"Oh, what the hell." She pulled off on the exit leading to the abbey.

It was her favorite time of day, right before dinnertime, and the waning sun threw rose highlights on the underbellies of the scudding clouds. Her mother used to call the color "sky blue pink."

She followed the sign that pointed toward the abbey, eventually drove through the open iron gate, and started up the long driveway to the monastery. She remembered sitting beside her father as he drove his old Ford Falcon up this same drive. What had drawn him here? His work with the monks always seemed to be something he just *did*—like paying the bills every month or mowing the lawn every week—which she never questioned. She would no more have asked why he went to the abbey than she would have asked why he took out the trash on Wednesday nights.

Why hadn't she talked to her parents about their faith? When she was young, Anne felt that religion was being forced on her, and as a college student she was relieved to be able to put all that aside. But now she wondered about what had been going on with her parents. If she had talked with them about their faith, maybe she'd believe in something today, instead of feeling that she was missing out on something other people had. She knew, though, that if she had asked, it probably would have turned into another heated discussion about why she didn't go to church.

She parked where Mark's truck had been just a few days before, in front of the chapel. Two other cars sat in the parking lot.

The stout wooden door to the chapel swung open silently. Once inside, Anne found herself on the other side of the wall that had annoyed her when Father Paul pointed it out. An elderly woman wearing a pale blue long-sleeved shirt, jeans, and sneakers knelt in the pew directly behind the low brick wall in the visitors' section. Anne sat in the last row. From there it was difficult to see the painting of Mary, which was against the wall on the side of chapel.

Anne craned her neck to get a better view. *It's absurd to have a visitors' section,* she thought. *What kind of church are they running here?*

She stood up and walked past the praying woman, who looked up just in time to watch Anne pass the low brick wall and enter the monks' section of the chapel. The woman sighed heavily, apparently annoyed to have her privacy disturbed.

Up close, the colors were more vivid than Anne remembered, brighter than on the card. Mary's dark red, almost brown, dress had a delicate white star that lay over her right shoulder. And Jesus wasn't wearing a white robe, as on the card, but a cream-colored one. His right hand formed a little peace sign, with his first two fingers pressed together. Mary wasn't looking at the child in her arms, though. She was looking out at Anne.

"Look at me," Mary seemed to say. "I know what you went through."

Someone coughed. And not the praying woman. Someone else. Anne's face flushed, and she froze in place. After a few uncomfortable seconds, she turned to her side and was horrified to see an ancient monk sitting in one of the back stalls, staring at her intently. She had obviously interrupted his prayer.

"Is that Annie?" he said in a cracked, hoarse voice.

"Yes," she said, "I'm Anne."

The old monk, bent over but with a nearly full head of steel-gray hair, grabbed the edge of the stall, pushed himself to a standing position, and smiled.

"Annie," he said, as he slowly made his way down the steps that led to the elevated back row. Anne felt as if she were seeing a ghost. He shuffled toward her.

"Father Edward?"

"In the flesh!" he said. "Well, what's left of it anyway." He smiled at her and showed her his large, misshapen teeth. She wondered if he still had bad breath.

"Let's go outside," he whispered. "We're not supposed to talk in here." He shuffled toward a door, dipped his fingers in the holy-water font, and blessed himself. Anne followed, and he led her into the same hallway she had been in with Mark and the abbot a few days ago. In the glassed-in garden, a slight breeze stirred the delicate pink blossoms of the cherry trees.

The hallways of the abbey were suffused with orange light from the setting sun. She wondered why it was so dark before and so light now, and realized that it had been raining the last time she was here.

"Oh, Annie," he said, as he gripped the arm of a wooden bench against a brick wall and slowly lowered himself onto the seat. He wasn't whispering. "The abbot told me you had come. I was so happy to hear it. It's so good to see you! And I'd recognize you *anywhere*. With your brown hair and that smile. But you've lost your freckles, haven't you?"

She blushed and smiled. There was hardly anyone around who remembered her as a girl—her parents were dead, and only a few cousins remained, scattered around Philly. They were supportive after the accident and in the weeks following, but after a few months she grew uncomfortable around them, not knowing what to say; she was also shocked and saddened by how much she resented their doting on their own, living children. Eventually, she stopped calling them.

"Your father was such a friend to us here—such a friend,"

said Father Edward emphatically. "So generous, doing our books for free for all those years."

Huh. She always assumed he had been paid.

"Yes," she said, "he was very generous in that way."

"What are you doing standing up? Sit down next to me. Right here, dear. And your mother! Your mother was a wonderful woman." He leaned in close to her on the bench and said, "They used to take me out to dinner every once in a while, and I used to enjoy playing hooky from the abbey."

Anne suppressed a smile when she noticed that he smelled like minty mouthwash. At some point over the past thirty years, someone must have told him about his breath.

"They took you out to dinner?" Anne asked.

"Oh yes," he said. "There was a wonderful restaurant near here called the Inn of the Four Falls." Anne remembered the place, situated near a busy highway, beside the sheer face of a rocky cliff down which four small waterfalls cascaded. "I loved the Clams Casino there." He closed his eyes in fond remembrance. "Once I had two helpings! Your mother got one, and I got one, and she gave me hers, because she knew I was embarrassed to order two for myself. Hah!"

How odd to sit here with a man she'd thought long dead, and one who spoke so freely about her parents. Suddenly, a window into her past opened up.

"Abbot Paul told me you had come, and I was so sorry that I didn't have a way of getting in touch with you. Where do you live?"

"Oh, just up the Blue Route. In Plymouth Meeting."

"Ah, not far at all. Was the other night the first time you've been back?" Without waiting for an answer he continued. "I've wondered all these years what had happened to you, Annie. I'm so sorry I couldn't find you. After your mother's funeral, I realized that I didn't know where you lived, and I didn't have your phone number. And back then it was difficult for us to use a phone, and we had only one phone book, and I didn't know your married name, and then I just lost touch. I'm so sorry, dear." Father Edward's regrets spilled out, and Anne was moved by his sadness.

She didn't know which of his comments to answer, so she started with the first one. "Yes, the other night was the first time I've been back in a long time."

Father Edward stared at her, smiling.

"I've always lived nearby, but I guess . . ." She didn't know how to say that she hadn't given the monastery much thought since her parents died.

"Oh, of course, you were busy," he said. "You have a *life*! Who would want to visit an old monk anyway?" He waved his hand, sweeping away any of her lingering unease.

Had he always been this kind? She began to see why her parents enjoyed his company. Father Edward hadn't stopped smiling from the moment he called her name in the chapel. He was smiling still, so happy to see her. She wondered if he was lonely. *Does anyone visit him?*

"Abbot Paul said you came by here with Mark the other

night. Is that right? Did you come for Vespers? Did you pray with us?"

"No, I didn't."

Father Edward waited expectantly to hear why she had come back, as if it were the most important thing in the world.

"Mark Matthews was giving me a ride because my car broke down, and then he remembered that he lost his cell phone." She laughed. "It's a little complicated."

Father Edward's cheerful face indicated that he was grateful for some conversation, even eager for a long story, so she told him the story of that evening, hoping it didn't sound too dismissive of the monastery—she'd come there by accident after all.

"It was Our Lady who brought you back," he said.

She stared at him.

"I saw you looking at the icon of Our Lady. Isn't it beautiful?"

"Yes."

"I've always liked the way she's holding Jesus," said Father Edward. "What do you like?"

Anne hadn't expected this sort of conversation, but Father Edward was so kind, and she found that she actually wanted to talk about this.

She told him how much she liked the way that Mary looked at the viewer in such a straightforward way. Mary was both tender with the baby and strong. She liked that combination.

"That's right," said Father Edward, who fixed his eyes on Anne as she spoke. "That's just the way Mary is. Tender and strong. And guess what? That icon is called Our Lady of Tenderness." He seemed grateful that Anne saw what he saw.

"So what have you been doing all these years? Are you married? Children? Are they in school anywhere near here? Catholic school, I hope!"

This time Anne refused to be led into tears. She shook her head sharply. "No, I'm afraid I'm divorced."

Father Edward said, "Oh, I'm sorry. That's a painful experience."

She paused. Finally she said, "And I had a son, but . . . he died a few years ago."

"Oh no!" Father Edward said, his eyes wide. "Oh, I'm so sorry!" He reached out, grabbed her hand, and squeezed hard. "What was his name?"

"Jeremiah."

Father Edward closed his eyes.

"Jeremiah," he said softly. "I will pray for him."

Anne nodded and felt her chest tightening. She would not cry.

"What happened to him?"

Anne told him the story. She had told it so often that she had memorized two versions, one short and one long. Tonight she used the short version: the accident, the hospital, the funeral. As she told the story, she stared into the cloister garden. Oddly, in the telling, even with all the details, she felt her emotions diminish. When she finished, she saw that Father Edward's eyes were filled with tears.

"I'm so sorry, Annie. I'm sure you miss him terribly. May he rest in peace."

She nodded.

The great bell rang out.

"Vespers," he said. "Would you like to join us?"

"No," she said, "I'll just sit here."

He released her hand. "I will pray for Jeremiah every day," he said. "But I'm sure he doesn't need my prayers. I'm sure your wonderful boy is already in heaven. And I'm sure he's been praying for you all this time, Annie."

She'd never thought of that before, and now she felt sadness and gratitude and guilt. She could have been praying for Jeremiah, and now he was praying for her. Now she was so confused that she didn't know what she believed. Anne dropped her head and fought the urge to cry.

"Oh, I'm so sorry," said Father Edward. "I always seem to say the wrong thing."

Monks materialized out of the many doorways in the hall and walked silently into the chapel, as the bell continued to toll.

"Annie," he whispered, "I'm sorry, but I have to go to Vespers. But I want to tell you something."

"Okay," she said.

"Don't forget that I'll be praying for your son and for you. And you come by here whenever you like. Ask for me too." Father Edward grabbed the arm of the bench, pushed himself up, and then bent over her as if speak to Anne again, but then straightened up. "God bless you," he said, and then walked slowly toward the chapel.

From the corner of her eye she saw the abbot approaching. He moved more swiftly than the other monks. As he drew nearer, he nodded and smiled, then stopped smiling when he saw her red eyes, and then smiled again.

"Welcome back," he said. "I'm glad to see you."

Anne nodded and smiled. He nodded back and entered the church.

She heard the monks move into their stalls and then settle in. A single organ note sounded.

"Let my evening prayer ascend before you, O Lord," sang a monk.

"And may your loving-kindness descend upon us," answered the others.

As she listened to the monks chanting their prayers, Anne wondered how she had arrived here. She hadn't planned on coming and was angry at herself for not being able to get that painting out of her mind. But now she was glad she had come. The music was beautiful, she liked the painting of Mary, and Father Edward was so friendly. It was almost like talking to her father again.

Then the monks began singing that song her father sang. She listened.

When Vespers ended, both Father Edward and the abbot returned to her bench. Before they had a chance to speak, she asked, "What was that last song you sang?"

"Oh, the Salve Regina?" said the abbot. "We sing that every night."

"My father used to hum that all the time. I never knew what it was."

Father Edward said, "You know, he used to love coming to Vespers and Compline. He prayed with us here all the time."

"I never knew that," she said. "I didn't know that at all."

13

Mark stood at Anne's front door the next Saturday morning wearing khaki shorts and a Boston Red Sox T-shirt.

"You know, you could get into trouble wearing that around here," she said.

He looked down at his chest and smiled. "Sometimes I don't even remember what I put on in the morning."

Anne laughed. "Men are lucky," she said. "At least you are."

Mark offered her a white letter-size envelope, blank, with no address or return address.

"What's this?"

"It's from Brad and his friends. To pay for the window. They promised me, or at least I *made* them promise me that they'd pay for it. So here you go."

She took the envelope and thought of how much she liked Brad. Always so good to Jeremiah, who had been a somewhat introverted child before he met the boy who would become his "best bud," as the two of them said. Brad—fearless, light-hearted, adventurous—unearthed a side of her son that she

84 ❖ James Martin, SJ

had never seen before, if she even knew it existed. One of her favorite memories of Jeremiah was when, at age eight or nine, he banged open the front door, raced into the kitchen, and shouted, "Mom! Brad asked me to play street hockey up at the school! Can I?" It was as if he had been given a free ticket to the World Series.

After the accident, although Brad was unfailingly polite, Anne could tell that he was avoiding her. And she found it hard to tell Brad—and never could find words that wouldn't make them both cry—that she missed her son's best friend. She missed having the two of them running through her living room, even if they were usually trailing mud, or in one case dog poop, on their shoes.

Privately, Brad's father, John, told her how much his son grieved after the funeral, locking himself in his room and throwing photos of himself and Jeremiah into the trash. John carefully fished them out of the trash can on the curb and kept them secretly, knowing that someday Brad would want his memories back. John said that Brad blamed himself for twisting Jeremiah's arm to ride his bike to the movies against his mother's wishes. Anne told her son's friend many times that she didn't blame him, but he seemed deaf to her forgiveness. And it was true: she knew how much Brad liked Jeremiah, and she didn't blame him at all. She was glad that she harbored no resentment against him. It simply wasn't there. One day she hoped to be able to tell him that.

Whenever Anne saw Brad, she felt an overpowering urge to hug him; he reminded her so much of Jeremiah. He was a living connection to her son. But at sixteen he was almost a man. The other day Anne had seen him driving his father's car. That meant that Jeremiah would have been driving too . . .

"You okay?" said Mark at the door.

Anne returned to the present. "Uh-huh," she said. "Fine. Just tired, that's all."

She looked at Mark's kind, open face and wondered whether she should tell him about her visit to the abbey. She wanted to tell someone. It was starting to feel weird to keep it secret. Plus it was really no big deal.

"Hey, I stopped by the abbey the other day on the way back from work."

Mark's eyebrows shot up toward his sandy hair. "You did?"

"You don't have to be so shocked. I went there when I was a kid, remember?" she said, then regretted her tone. If she had surprised herself by visiting the abbey, why wouldn't it surprise him?

"Yeah," she continued. "It was pretty interesting seeing P&J after all those years. Did I tell you that my father had worked for them as an accountant? Did their books?"

Mark nodded.

"They're pretty nice there. And I ran into an old monk who knew my father."

"They're not just pretty nice—they're great. I love those guys." Now it was Anne's turn to be surprised.

"Sure," he said, "some of them are a pain in the ass, but I really like them on the whole. Who's the one your father knew?"

"Father Edward."

Mark threw his head back and laughed. "Oh, Father Ed! He's a stitch. Do you know he's so forgetful that when we were helping him clean out his room last year we found about a hundred dollars in loose cash?"

"Are they supposed to have all that money?" asked Anne. "Aren't they monks?"

"Yeah, they take vows of poverty, so they don't have any money of their own, and any gifts they get—you know, cash and stuff—they turn over to the community. Anyway, Father Ed sometimes gets cash gifts from his family for Christmas and his birthday, twenty-dollar bills and the like, and do you know where he puts them?"

Anne shook her head.

"He uses them as bookmarks!"

"What, he uses twenty-dollar bills as bookmarks?" Anne said. "Like some millionaire? So much for poverty."

"No, no," Mark said, "That's just it. Father Ed doesn't care about money. He's really, you know, pretty free that way. I mean, he usually turns it in, but sometimes he just . . . forgets. Money just isn't something he thinks about."

Anne didn't know how she felt about that. Was that being free, or stupid?

"Anyway," Mark said, seeing her apparent disapproval, "Father Ed's a great guy. He's really nice to me. And so are Father Paul and Brother Robert. Brother Robert's my favorite though. Always telling me he'll pray for me, and I figure, hey, it can't hurt."

"No," said Anne. "I guess not."

She thanked Mark for the envelope and started to shut the door just as Sunshine tore down the hall and hurled himself at the doorway in a vain effort to attack the stranger. Mark bent down, narrowed his eyes, and glowered at Sunshine, which enraged the tiny dog. Anne waved to Mark from behind the screen door, and then shut it.

"Shut up, you demon!" she said to the dog, who barked once, insolently, as if he knew that Mark would hear.

Inside the envelope was a single sheet of unlined paper. When Anne unfolded it, cash rained onto the living room carpet: several twenty-dollar bills, a few tens, and two fives. Brad and his friends had probably pooled their resources to come up with the payment for the window.

She bent down, picked up the money, and read the note.

In terrible handwriting was written, "I'm sorry."

14

"Get out of here!" Kerry said when Anne explained why she couldn't go out for a drink after work. "You're going to the *monastery*? Since when are you so religious?" Kerry and Anne were seated at a faux-wood conference table at the end of the working day, with financial records spread before them—a maelstrom of bills, receipts, income statements, balance sheets, and bank reconciliations.

"I'm not," she said, immediately regretting telling her friend. "I'm just visiting a friend of my father's, an old monk who lives there."

"They creep me out up there," said Kerry. "No sex for your whole life? Praying all the time? Thanks, but no thanks. On the other hand, their jam's pretty awesome. Yum. Pick me up a few jars, will you? I like the blueberry preserves."

Initially Anne was inclined to defend the monks, but then realized that she agreed with Kerry, at least on a few points. The last time she was at the abbey she caught herself thinking, *What do they do all day?* Still, she knew enough not to get into a religious discussion with Kerry, who had little time for anything religious. When anyone in the office mentioned the word "church," usually on Mondays, Kerry would sigh heavily and roll her eyes.

For the past few days, Anne felt crushed by work. Her firm had recently picked up a new client who needed an immediate audit, thanks to an embezzling business manager. Anne could never understand how so many people could steal from their employers, but she saw enough of it to know that it happened frequently. This latest disaster was typical. Kerry and Anne were auditing a firm whose business manager set up false companies that billed his company for services that were never rendered. It came to light only when the business manager bragged about his malfeasance to another employee, oddly proud that he had tricked the CEO for so long. Working on those jobs was satisfying, because Anne felt she could help set things right, but it also made her feel almost unclean. That audit made her want to visit the monastery.

After assuring Kerry she wasn't going to become a nun, Anne halfheartedly organized the financial records she had been reviewing, grabbed her jacket, piled into her car, and set off toward the abbey.

As she drove along the Blue Route, it occurred to her that she was actually looking forward to this. Visiting Father Edward was the right thing to do, a kind of payback for all the kindnesses people had shown her after Jeremiah's death—the visits, the phone calls, the flowers, the cards, the casseroles. The day after the funeral, when she told Jeremiah's father that she wouldn't accept any more food or flowers, he said, "It's their way of showing you love. You have to let them love you like this." Eddie wasn't often right, but she knew he was then.

In some odd way, those many kindnesses and her visit to Father Edward seemed connected—a cycle of giving, receiving, and being grateful.

The sun hung low in the sky when Anne arrived at the front gate. On the long driveway, she passed a woman with her head bowed, walking slowly. Farther up, an elderly man strolled around aimlessly, and under the arches of the church's portico a few more people were huddled together, chatting. Was she intruding on some religious conference? She still had no idea what happened at the abbey other than a few simple facts: the monks prayed, went to Mass, made jam, and didn't have sex.

And, again, she had come unprepared: she had no clue how to find Father Edward. A few hours earlier at work, she had started to call the abbey, but then didn't, remembering that the monks didn't have phones in their rooms. The only number listed on their website was for the jam factory, which she didn't want, and the guest house, whatever that was. She had left a message at the guest house, but didn't know if it would find its way to Father Edward.

The church loomed at the top of the driveway. Confused, Anne circled back around the parking lot, looking for something indicating where the monks lived. She flushed, embarrassed and angry that she had come without knowing where she was going. "Shit," she said aloud. Then she noticed, on a post stuck into the ground, a small wooden sign with red lettering that read "Guest House."

She followed a gravel road to a one-story stone cottage whose mullioned windows, red wooden door, and slate roof made it look as if it belonged to a hobbit. The few people wandering along the driveway peered into her car as she passed. *Nosy,* she thought.

The abbey's great bell began to chime in the tall gray steeple. Like anxious deer, the men and women looked up, turned toward the church, and fast-walked up the driveway. Vespers.

Anne rang the bell at the guest-house door. No answer. Maybe all the monks were at Vespers. She pushed the door open to find an elderly woman with dark tousled hair sitting at the desk.

"Oh," she said, as she slowly stood. "I was just about to open it!"

Anne stepped into a small, red-tiled foyer carpeted with worn oriental rugs and crammed with bookcases. One bookcase was entirely taken up with a display of the abbey's jams and jellies. Beside it stood a spindly metal rack of note cards. Most cards featured colorful photos of the monastery throughout the year—the abbey church covered with snow, springtime blossoms in the cloister garden, butterflies on the lilac bushes by the driveway, a stand of red-leaved maple trees in the valley. Several cards showed the image of Mary inside the church. One was the card that Father Paul had given her that first night.

On the elderly woman's desk was a small sign that read, "Guest Master." Anne suppressed a smile: it sounded vaguely risqué. Then she wondered why the monks needed such a big place for guests. Was this where their families stayed?

"Are you here for a retreat?" the woman asked.

Anne laughed. "Oh no!" She realized that this might sound insulting, so she quickly added, "I'm here to see Father Edward. Is he around?"

"I'm Maddy," said the woman, sticking out her hand. "The monks just went to Vespers, but we got your message today, and he's looking forward to seeing you. You can sit here for a bit until prayers are over, if you'd like."

Sighing heavily, Anne sat down on a high-backed wooden chair and examined some magazines on a coffee table before her: *America, Commonweal, U.S. Catholic, First Things, Liguorian, St. Anthony Messenger*. She dimly remembered seeing her parents read some of these and flipped through one of them. Lots of photos of the pope, various cardinals and bishops, people in the developing world, and happy Americans smiling as they left Sunday Mass. She tossed each magazine back on the table, one by one, then took out her cell phone, and began checking her e-mail.

"Excuse me," said Maddy, "I'm afraid you can't use your cell phone here. We try to keep things quiet."

More rules. Another reason she didn't go to church. Then she figured that since this woman undoubtedly knew what went on here, she'd satisfy her curiosity.

"Can I ask you a stupid question?" asked Anne. As the words came out of her mouth she anticipated Maddy's response. She was not disappointed.

"There are no stupid questions."

"Okay," she said. "What do the monks do all day? Other than pray and make jam?"

Maddy laughed. "Well, that's a full day, if you ask me. Between prayer, community business, and working in the jam factory, some of these guys are busier than I am. And I'm pretty busy."

"So," said Anne, feeling that her question had been politely avoided, "they do . . . what, exactly?"

"Oh, I'm sorry," said Maddy. "Well, their day is pretty full. I guess you know they start their prayers at three thirty and—"

"What—three thirty?"

"Yes, that's Vigils, and then—"

"Three thirty in the *morning*?"

"Yes," Maddy said, relishing Anne's surprise. "Then comes some personal prayer and reading until about four, I think. Then they get dressed, I guess, and have breakfast. After that, there's Lauds, which is their morning prayer, and then Mass, and then . . ." She trailed off. "You know, I always forget the exact schedule. Wait a minute . . ."

She reached into a drawer and pulled out a well-worn sheet of paper headed with the word "Horarium."

"Here," Maddy said. "*Horarium* means 'the hours.' It's their schedule of the day. Take a look."

Maddy led Anne through the day. Before Mass, the monks prayed the Angelus, whatever that was. They said that prayer three times a day, said Maddy. Then they worked either in the jam factory or in jobs around the house until noon.

"So what kind of things would they do?" asked Anne.

"Well, a few work in the jam factory, both in the business office and on the factory floor. And of course they tend the gardens and harvest vegetables, and there's lots of cleaning to do, with the bathrooms and all that. And then some of them work in the kitchen; and then there's a novice director, a director of the young monks in formation, which is their word for training. And some of them do spiritual direction for people outside the house; and there's the sacristan, who takes care of the church; and then the infirmarian, who takes care of the monks in the infirmary; and then the guest master . . ."

"Isn't that you?" asked Anne.

"Oh no!" Maddy laughed. "*I'm* not the guest master. That's Brother James. I just help out and sub for him when they're in chapel. They call me the 'sub–guest master.' Abbot Paul calls me the 'guest mistress' or sometimes the 'mistress of guests,' which makes me laugh."

If Maddy hadn't been focused on the page, she would have seen Anne smiling. That last title sounded even more suggestive.

"So then," she said, "here's the rest of the day." Midmorning prayer in the workplace, and then Sext, which is another prayer in the chapel, then their big meal at twelve thirty, followed by washing dishes. After that, a rest or a walk. At two o'clock came mid-afternoon prayer followed by more work. Then they could pray (Anne thought, *Pray again?*); rest (*That's what I'd be doing*); or exercise. She pictured them jogging around the grounds in their long black-and-white habits.

Vespers she knew. That was the prayer she always seemed to be interrupting, at five thirty. After that came a light "supper," which sounded pleasantly old-fashioned. Followed by more prayer and reading and finally Compline, or night prayer, during which they prayed the Salve Regina.

"What's that?"

"What's what?"

"This"—she pointed to the page. "Salve Regina." Anne pronounced the first word like an ointment—*sav.*

"Oh," said Maddy, "the Sahl-vay Ray-jee-nuh. It's a song to Mary. It goes like this." She hummed a few bars.

Anne was again startled to hear the tune her father had loved. She had forgotten the name, though Father Paul had told her that first night.

"Oh, yes, I like that song," said Anne. "What's it mean?"

Maddy paused. "You know, I don't *know.* It's about Mary— that much I know. *Salve Regina* means 'Hail Queen.' But, you know . . . Isn't that funny? I'm not really sure what the rest of it means." She furrowed her brow, disappointed in herself, then laughed. "I only know it in Latin I guess. Anyway, that's how they end their day, with that song. Then the abbot blesses them, and they go to bed, and the 'Great Silence' begins. They're supposed to be quiet until three thirty."

"And then they can talk?"

"Well, not really. Not a lot at least. I'm not really sure. They talk at various points during the day of course, but they try to keep silence, and sometimes they even use sign language."

Anne looked upon the schedule in its entirety. It seemed a daunting way to live.

"That's a lot of prayer," she said. "And work, I guess."

"*Ora et labora,*" said Maddy cheerfully.

Anne stared at her.

"Prayer and work."

Maddy looked at Anne with something resembling pity, or so Anne thought. "You know, a few years ago I made a retreat here after I lost my job. I didn't know what I was going to do. My husband and I needed my salary, since he's on disability now, which doesn't cover a whole lot. After a few months of sitting around the house, I felt like I was at the end of my rope. And worst of all, God felt completely absent. I felt like saying, 'Where are you, God?' You know what I mean?"

Anne nodded.

"My husband saw a notice in our parish bulletin about a weekend retreat for women, and he kept nagging me until I went. Anyway, I just fell in love with this place. I mean just *look* at it." She gestured toward a window that framed a view of the abbey church under a setting sun and vermilion sky.

"Abbot Paul was so gentle on that retreat, and he listened, I mean really listened, like no man ever had to me—not even my husband, whom I love." Maddy stared into space.

"I love these guys," Maddy said firmly. "They've helped me so much. And they love me back. At least it feels like they do. Not all of them of course—I think I drive a few of them crazy. And, frankly, a few of them drive *me* crazy. But, you know, when you think about it, that's not such a bad way to live. Praying and working and loving other people as friends, and thinking about God all the time, right? Not so bad, huh?"

"No," Anne said, surprising herself. "Not so bad at all."

15

Father Paul walked into the guest house and grinned when he saw Anne. "Ah, is this a new retreatant?"

"No, Father," said Maddy. "She's here to see Father Edward."

"Yes," said Paul. "I was just kidding. Though maybe one day you could come on retreat here."

Anne didn't know what to say, so she said, "Maybe . . . I guess." She realized that the nosy people looking into her car were probably on retreat.

Paul took Anne's hand with two hands and welcomed her. "Father Edward told me that you were coming, but he's not feeling very well today."

"Anything serious?"

"No, no, just old age. That, and we buried one of his good friends this week, Father George. They both entered as novices together, about fifty years ago. So that really affected him. Father George was the last member of his novitiate class. Father Edward's very upset that he can't meet with you, but he really needs his rest. Abbot's orders. But he asked me to look after you and make sure you were doing well. Can I at least get you a cup of coffee?"

Anne was annoyed that she had come all this way and wished she had known that the priest was sick. *What a waste of time,* she thought. *Why didn't the monks have their own phones anyway? What if someone needed to reach them in an emergency? Did they have to rely on a note from Maddy eventually finding its way to them?* Life in the monastery seemed consciously, almost willfully, archaic.

Still, she liked Father Edward. Father Paul was nice too. He had been so kind to her that day outside the cloister garden. So she agreed to the cup of coffee.

"And you *should* come for a retreat," said Maddy.

Anne nodded politely. "Thanks for telling me what the monks do."

"Oh!" said Paul. "I'd like to hear about *that*! What do we do here, O Mistress of Guests?"

Maddy chuckled. "I was just showing her the Horarium, that's all."

After thanking Maddy, Paul escorted Anne through the halls of the guest house. As with the main building of the monastery, the guest house was arranged around a cloister garden, this one more modest but still beautiful, filled with skillfully clipped rhododendron and azalea bushes. Over the doors of the guest rooms were oval signs reading "St. Ignatius," "St. Bernard," "St. Anne," and several other names Anne remembered from Sunday school. Each sign, which featured a depiction of a saint, appeared to have been hand painted and

lettered, but years ago; the colors were faded almost to the
point of transparency.

These were the retreatants' bedrooms, said Paul, each of
them named after a saint. "It's easier to remember names than
numbers, plus the retreatants have a patron saint during their
retreat."

They passed through a narrow, brick-lined hallway and entered the monastery. As they walked through the long halls,
the abbot provided a running commentary.

"So the retreatants come and spend anywhere from a
weekend to eight days with us. They eat in the retreatants'
dining room and usually join us for our prayers, and for Mass
of course. Some of them get up for Lauds, but most of them
only make it to the later prayers. And we're happy to have
them. Hospitality is part of our life here. The rest of the day is
their own, for prayer of course, but also spiritual reading. And
they can get spiritual direction if they want from one of the
monks . . .

"This is the kitchen, as you can see, and here's our wonderful chef, Christian. Who's from Paris, believe it or not.
We have an actual French chef. *Bonsoir,* Christian, what's for
dinner? Really? Great. You've not forgotten about Brother
James's special diet for his little, um, procedure tomorrow,
have you? Thank you . . .

"Okay, so obviously here's the cloister garden, which you
can see through those windows. Isn't it lovely this time of
year? Of course every time of year is lovely here, as far as
I'm concerned. And that door right there—no, that one over

there—leads to the infirmary, where the sick monks stay. That's where Father Edward is right now, but we pray it's not for too long . . .

"And way down this hall is the entrance to the church, where you've already been of course. You know, you're always welcome to drop by and pray whenever you want. Here's the library, which I guess you can tell from all those books in there. That's Father Brian at the desk, our house librarian, no doubt trying to impose some sort of order on a carton of books that was donated the other day. And outside this door here is the cemetery, where we'll all end up one day. And here's my office."

In their long walk, they passed only a handful of monks, and all of them were silent, though some nodded discretely as they passed the abbot. And of course there was no noise coming from any radios or televisions or computers. Or anything. The silence enveloped Anne. It was like something she could touch. Like a blanket.

Paul led her into his office and invited her to sit in one of the red wingback chairs that flanked a small coffee table. Paneled in dark wood, the abbot's office contained an immense pine desk with an old swivel office chair behind it, and two tall pine bookcases stuffed with books. Several small framed photos stood on a putty-colored metal file cabinet.

On one wall was a large crucifix: the smooth ivory body of Jesus gleamed against a rough ebony cross. A large print of the image of Mary from the abbey church hung over the abbot's desk, which was stacked with piles of folders and papers.

"I like that picture," said Anne.

"Ah yes," said Paul. "What do you like about it?"

Anne moved closer to the abbot's desk and gazed at the image.

"Mmm . . . I like the way Mary is looking out at me . . ." She caught herself. "I mean, looking out at the viewer. It's like she's not afraid to look out and show everyone what she's experienced."

"And what do you think she's experienced?"

Anne knew what the abbot was doing—trying to get her to talk about her own experiences—but she was grateful for his concern and so accepted the tacit invitation. "She had to suffer a great deal." Though her answer was calculated, saying it saddened her nonetheless.

"Yes," said Paul. "A great deal." He paused for a few seconds while Anne continued to gaze at the image.

"Oh, I forgot the coffee!" he said suddenly. "How do you take it?"

"Surprise me."

After Paul left, Anne settled comfortably into one of the chairs and exhaled. She stared at the still-setting sun through the window. After a minute, she popped up, walked over to the bookshelves, and began examining their contents. Mostly they were formidable tomes on Jesus, the Trinity, Mary, church history, monastic life, and prayer. Feeling nosy, she perused the neat rows of framed photos on his file cabinet.

Most were reproductions of religious paintings—including a Salvador Dalí painting of Jesus floating up to heaven, which

Anne thought creepy. Many were photos of an elderly couple Anne supposed were Paul's parents—both tall, both with glasses. And three showed Paul himself: arm in arm, laughing, with capped and gowned friends at a college graduation, perhaps his own; dressed as a priest and kneeling before a bishop whose hands were placed on the crown of Paul's head; and pouring water over a baby's head. The photographer had caught the precise moment of baptism; Anne could pick out the individual water droplets as they fell from Paul's hand and were about to land on the infant's pale, perfectly round head.

Her eye was drawn again to the image of Mary on the wall, and she stared at it for a long while. This time she seemed to say not "I know," but "I want to know."

Mary seemed to look at her with the eyes of a friend who was waiting for her to talk. Like the time she went out to dinner in Center City with Kerry on her first day back from work after Jeremiah's death. Anne said she needed to blow off some steam, and Kerry took her to her favorite Thai restaurant and announced that it was her treat. "Ask for anything you want."

An hour later, looking down into her third gin and tonic, Anne said, "You know what?" She was about to say that she couldn't concentrate at all on work. That she wasn't sure what she was doing half the time. And that all she thought about, every moment of every day, was Jeremiah.

Kerry reached across the table, grabbed Anne's hand, and squeezed it tight.

"What?" said Kerry.

When Anne looked up from her drink she saw Kerry's kind face, ready to hear whatever Anne wanted to say. After the accident, Kerry was ready to hear about pain and sadness, ready to hear about grief and loss, ready to hear about anger and fear. Ready to hear anything Anne wanted to say. Ready.

That was the look she now saw on Mary's face.

16

Anne's back was turned when Father Paul entered the room, so he did surprise her.

"I like that image too," he said.

"Oh!" Anne had moved behind his desk and was examining the icon. "I didn't mean to take over your office. I'm afraid you caught me snooping around a bit. Sorry."

"When I entered the novitiate here, I was pretty lonely for my family," said Paul, settling into one of the chairs. He handed Anne a heavy white cup filled with creamy coffee, and she took the chair opposite Paul. "My father had died a few years before, and I was close to my mother. So I told my novice director all that. And you know what he said?"

Anne prepared to hear something absurd.

"My novice director said that I should ask Mary to pray for me and pray for my mother."

Anne smiled. "I thought you were going to tell me that he told you that Mary should *be* your mother."

"Ha!" said Paul. "I would have laughed if he said that. Come to think of it, my mom would have too."

Anne and Paul then talked about their mothers, who, as it happened, went to the same high school. Both sets of parents were married in the same church, though a decade apart. People from Philadelphia tended not to move around much, so these kinds of coincidences rarely surprised Anne. But it increased her affection for Paul. He was only slightly older than Anne, so they also knew a few of the same people, the same places, and liked the same spots at the Jersey shore—though she was disappointed when she discovered that he was only a tepid Phillies fan. "It's hard to follow the games without a TV or radio in my room," said Paul.

When she asked what first drew him to the abbey, he told her about his Catholic upbringing and the story of how he once came here on a high-school retreat and was "bowled over" by the place. The idea of entering the monastery endured through his years at college and beyond. But it wasn't the silence that kept him here. There was something else. Something more, he said.

"God keeps me here."

Anne sipped the coffee. "Wow. Mark was right. This coffee is awesome. Do you make that here too?"

"No, just jam, I'm afraid. Brother Robert buys the rest of what we need at the supermarket."

Anne stared into her cup, deciding whether to venture a question. "What do you mean when you say God keeps you here?"

"Well, I know it sounds a bit mystical, but it's really quite practical. It means that I'm happy here."

"That's it?" Anne said. "Being happy keeps you here?"

"That . . . and other things," said Paul. "When I was a young man, twenty-five at the time, I felt this great pull to the monastic life. And that was the way God was working in my life—through that pull. It didn't seem to make much sense at the time. I mean, no one in my family was a monk or anything like that. And the only priests we knew were the ones we saw during Mass on Sundays. But in another way, it was the only thing that *did* make sense. I just couldn't get this place out my head. And when I finally came here for the novitiate, I don't think I had ever been happier. It just fit me. The first year was just lovely. I liked the community life, and the stability, and oh, how I loved all that beautiful singing! Then, after novitiate, I made my vows and promised God I'd stay here. So you could also say that what keeps me here is that I told God I would stay. But God's also been very faithful to me here."

"Meaning?"

"Meaning . . . that God's given me the grace to stay, and he's given me a lot of happiness in the past twenty-five years. More than I could have expected. And in ways I could never have imagined. It's not the perfect life. Not by any means. We certainly have our share of problems. And unlike in other settings, if you don't get along with someone, you can't move—and neither can he. We take a vow of stability in addition to the other vows. So it's not perfect. But I would say . . . it's perfect for me. So I see God in all of that."

Anne stared at her coffee cup again. This was already the longest religious conversation she had ever had, except for the arguments she had with her parents after she stopped going to church.

"Yeah," she said. "I'm not so big on God right now."

Paul paused. "I can understand that, I think."

Anne said nothing, alarmed that she was being drawn deeper into a discussion about religion. But she also felt a growing curiosity. It was as if a part of her wanted to talk about God. Weird but exciting, like discussing something taboo.

"You know," said Paul, "Father Edward was very upset when he heard about your son's death. I don't think I'm breaking confidence to tell you that he offered Mass for your son the next day."

"He did?"

Paul nodded. He looked at her intently.

"That was very thoughtful," she said quietly. "Please tell him I said thank you."

"I hope you'll be able to do that yourself soon."

Anne stared out the window at the remaining light in the sky, which had now turned violet. "So can I ask you something?"

"Feel free."

"How can you believe in a God who lets these things happen?" Anger rushed into her heart and tightened her lips. Now that she had said it, had let it out, some of the fury she experienced after Jeremiah's death returned.

That her rage at God surfaced only one time after the accident surprised Anne. She thought she'd be angrier at God. On the other hand, maybe that meant she didn't believe in God any longer. Around the time she started college, she drifted away from the church or, as she thought of it, the church drifted away from her. No women priests? Boring homilies? No birth control? No thanks. During her senior year at Haverford she stopped going to Mass, to the consternation of her mother, and her father even more. Christmas and Easter were the exceptions. Her parents insisted on that, and so she went to Mass with them twice a year. To keep the peace.

Sometimes Anne missed it. Parts of it. She liked some of the songs they sang in Sunday school, finding them comforting. The Rosary that her father carried in his pocket and the statues of the saints that her mom kept in her parents' bedroom were talismans of a more certain time in her life. But what did her father see in the church, she used to wonder, and why did he spend so much time with the monks? (The answer to that second question was becoming clearer.) For the most part, she was pleased to be rid of her faith, which she considered a vestige of a childish way of viewing the world. Overall, it was an encumbrance.

But the day after Jeremiah's funeral, after her ex-husband's car pulled out of the driveway and the house was finally empty for the first time since the accident, Anne found herself in the bathroom, sobbing, barely able to catch her breath. Kneeling on the cold white tile floor, wedged between the sink and the bathtub, she heard herself scream, "I hate you, God! Why did you *do* this?" Anne shouted that question over and over and over, until eventually, hearing no answer, she stopped shouting. In the end she stood up, dried her tears and blew her nose, looked at herself in the mirror, and said, "Screw it."

She told Paul this story now, dispassionately.

The abbot listened intently. Then he stared into the swirls of milk in his cup and paused for a long time.

"It's okay for us to hate God at a time like that," he said. "It's natural. And God can take it. And if you're shouting at God, that means you're still in relationship with God. That's important."

Anne continued to peer through the window, still unable to look at Paul.

"I think I still hate God," she said quietly. "I hate him for taking away my son. Sometimes I say . . . sometimes I say to myself . . ." She paused. "You're not going to like this."

Paul said nothing.

"Sometimes I say . . . I wish I were dead."

Paul nodded silently. Anne took this as permission to continue.

"Sometimes I think of Jeremiah so much that I don't think I can live anymore. I mean, sometimes I don't think I can survive the sadness. I don't know how else to describe it, but it's like I can't breathe. I can't believe it's possible to be so . . . sad. And sometimes I feel like everything is pointless. It's getting better, I guess. A little. I mean, it's not as bad as it was." She paused.

"I think about what I should have done to stop him going to the movies that night. I think about the way he looked in the hospital. Oh, *God*! I think about his funeral that day. And you know what I think about most of all?"

Paul waited.

"I think about what he would be *doing now*!" she said, her voice rising. "I think about that when I see his friends riding their bikes and laughing and playing baseball. The other day some of the kids hit a baseball through Mark's window, and Mark was so worried about it, and when he told me, you know what I was thinking? You know what I was *thinking*?"

She was trying to get the words out through her sobs now.

"What?"

She shouted, "How I wanted *Jeremiah* to be with them! What I would *give* to have *him* be able to do something stupid like that! To play ball! To break windows! Instead of being *dead*!"

The last word rang through the halls of the abbey. Paul's face fell, and tears filled his eyes.

"Sometimes I want to die," she said. "I want to die so that I can end all this, and maybe, maybe . . . be with him again. But I'm not even sure about that."

Paul let her words fill the room. "You loved him so much," he said.

"Yes," she said quietly.

Silence descended upon them.

"More than I can describe," she said.

"And I'm sure he loved you."

"Yes."

"I'm so sorry, Anne," he said. "I'm so sorry about Jeremiah."

Anne wiped her red eyes with the back of her left hand. On the coffee table was a pink box of tissues, which Paul pushed closer to her. She pulled one from the box. "Thank you."

The abbey bell intoned the hour.

"That's pretty," she said, wiping away her tears. "It must be nice to live here."

"Yes, it is."

He waited for a long while and finally said, "How do you think God sees you right now?"

Anne looked at him, confused.

"How would I know?" she said. "I mean . . . I don't know."

Paul paused for a moment, staring at the faded oriental carpet. Then he looked up. Anne saw his gaze rest on the image of Mary.

"Well," he said. "In that case, how do you think Mary looks at you right now?"

Anne sucked in air and looked at the image. "Oh," she said, with a frown. Then more tears came. "Oh, I think she would feel sorrow for me." She pulled another tissue from the box. She could feel Paul watching her. He put his elbows on the arms of his chair, steepled his hands, and closed his eyes.

"That touches you deeply, doesn't it?" he said.

"Yes," she said quietly and looked out at the sky. With the last traces of day gone, its hue was dark violet. Only a few lavender clouds were visible. This time of day always made her feel calm, as if all the hard work was over.

"It's nice to think about that," she said. "When you just said that, it made me feel, I don't know, less alone. I think Mary would understand me . . . and feel sorrow for me. Her son died too. I was just thinking about that the other day. She would understand me. Especially if she was like that." She motioned to the picture on Paul's wall.

"She was like that," he said. "And is like that. Close to Jesus to the last."

"What did you say?"

"Close to Jesus to the last," he said. "It's from a prayer about Mary that I like. In fact, I think it was on the back of the card I gave you the other day."

Anne opened her lips to speak, but then fell silent.

"Can I ask you something?" said Paul.

Anne nodded.

"If Mary feels sorrow for you, do you think her son could too?"

She had never thought of them together like that. Like two human beings who could feel sorrow for someone.

"And if her son does, don't you think God could too?"

Anne stared at her coffee. "I don't know," she said. "What do you think?"

"God is mercy," he said. "So I think God looks down on you with the greatest love imaginable. And what does God see right now? A loving mother who misses her child more than she can say. And more than I can know. God is all mercy, and loves you, Anne. And God understands your anger and your pain and, in a way, God loves you even *more* for all that. God loves us more when we're hurting, the way . . . the way that *you* loved Jeremiah when he was hurting or struggling."

Anne sobbed. "Oh, God, I *miss* him . . . so much!"

"I can see that. God sees that too."

Then she wiped her eyes and looked directly at Paul. "So what do I do with all this?"

"You can continue to be honest with God about all of this. Why not tell God how you feel?"

"You mean by praying? I don't really pray."

"I think you do. That prayer you said to God was a good one, you know."

Anne laughed through her tears. "You mean when I said, 'I hate you'? My father would have been horrified to hear me say that."

"But it was honest. Of course we can't say that all the time. No more than we could say that to a friend all the time. But it expressed what you were feeling at the time," said Paul. "And God wants your honesty. Just like any good friend would want that."

Anne looked at the image of Mary.

"Lots of people think they're not allowed to be angry at God," he continued, shifting in the chair. "But anger is a natural part of life. It says we're human. Jesus was angry. Remember? He gets angry at some of the people of his time. He calls them a 'faithless and perverse generation.' He gets angry at the merchants in the Temple . . ."

"But he was God," said Anne.

"He was human too. So he got angry. As you can. You can tell God how you feel. God's been handling people's anger for a long time. Do you know Psalm 13?"

Anne smiled slightly. "No."

Paul said, "How long, O Lord?"

"Excuse me?"

"'How long, O Lord?' is how Psalm 13 begins. It's the cry of someone who feels abandoned by God." He rose, took a step toward his desk, picked up a worn Bible, flipped through it, and began to read.

How long, O Lord? Will you forget me forever?
How long will you hide your face from me?
How long must I bear pain in my soul,
and have sorrow in my heart all day long?
How long shall my enemy be exalted over me?

"That's a psalm?"

"Mmm hmm. There's a whole group of psalms called 'lament psalms,' which are basically people being sad or angry or disappointed in God. Calling out for help. The next line is really powerful. We sing it several times a year here. Some translations say, 'Consider and answer me, God.' But another one says, 'Look at me! Answer me!'"

Anne didn't know what to say. So she said nothing. She felt a weird connection to whoever wrote that psalm.

"Answer me," she said. "That's how I feel."

"Why don't you try telling God how you feel?"

"How do I do that?"

"Well, you could just imagine yourself talking with God. Sometimes people imagine themselves in God's presence in a general way. Or sometimes they imagine that God is sitting in a chair next to them."

"Seriously?"

"Okay," said Paul. "Maybe you could write God a letter. Maybe you could write your own lament psalm."

"Doesn't God know what I think already?"

"Doesn't a good friend know what you think already?" said Paul. "Didn't your friends know how you felt at Jeremiah's funeral? And didn't you share your feelings with them anyway? It's part of being in a relationship with someone."

Anne thought about Kerry's ability to listen.

The abbey bell rang out several times. "That's Compline," said Paul. "Would you like to join us?"

"No, no." She rose from her chair and looked outside at the sky, where a sliver of a moon sailed over the church steeple. "Thanks for your time. Would you tell Father Edward I'd still like to see him sometime?"

"I promise," said Paul. He opened a closet door and pulled something from a shelf. "Take these," he said, handing her a gift box of jams. "If you get hungry writing that letter, you can have some of these blueberry preserves."

17

Father Paul was happy to have met with Anne. Though he enjoyed life at the abbey, he treasured opportunities for pastoral work. Of course, as Father David, one of the former abbots, reminded Paul after his election, any time an abbot spent with his brother monks—visiting the sick and elderly men in the infirmary, encouraging young novices during times of confusion, advising monks in the jam factory on management decisions; in fact, any time that he spent with a brother at the abbey—was pastoral work.

"You know what I mean," said Paul. "It's good to talk with people on the outside."

"Agreed," said Father David cheerfully. "Plus, talking with seculars reminds us that monks aren't the only ones who have problems."

But it was more than that. Paul liked helping people who didn't have as many invitations to see God in their lives. Monastic life made it easier to find God. Not that he believed monks were holier than anyone else. Actually, he felt that the opposite was more often true.

A monk's whole day was built around praising God. "Monastic life makes it hard to forget about God," his novice director told him. But people on the outside faced pressures that sometimes made it harder to remember God. For one thing, there were the constraints of time. That's why Paul believed mothers and fathers and doctors and lawyers and teachers and janitors—at least many of them—were holier than monks. They had to make room for God in a world that often crowded out God.

That was another reason he liked talking to visitors. Paul could see such holiness in them. And it consistently amazed him, no matter how many times he saw it, to watch how God worked so personally, so intimately, with people. He could see how God tailored his approach to fit each individual. In one person God might work through a close relationship, in another through a book, in another through prayer, in others through music, nature, dance, children, coworkers, or art.

Paul knew this was a grace: he saw God in nearly everyone he met. As he did in Anne, who seemed to be drawn to God even if she wasn't aware of that yet. Even in her grief, Anne seemed open to what Paul had to say.

Mark was another person whom Paul felt he had been able to help, if in a small way. When Mark started working at the abbey, he seemed frustrated and lost. His frustration sometimes made him taciturn, reserved, and at times even dejected. Paul wondered if the loss of his job at the architecture firm in Boston had led Mark into a mild depression.

In time, Mark began to open up to Paul, mainly when the

two of them were on their way to do something else. Mark, an active, occasionally jittery man, rarely paused long enough for the kind of in-depth conversation Paul was accustomed to having with the monks. On the way to examining a rotten tree that needed chopping down, en route to checking on a leaky faucet in the dormitory, or while helping him set up for a big celebration in the refectory, Mark would share some of his life with Paul.

Mark's questions were usually about two topics: work and relationships. Misfortune in his professional life—losing his job had sapped his self-confidence—seemed the most important concern for Mark. But for Paul the deeper question was one of loneliness. Mark dated a lot of women and, though he only occasionally alluded to it, slept around a lot. Sometimes he got drunk in Center City and fell into bed with whatever woman he had met that night. Paul prayed that he could help Mark see that whatever job he did, whether as an architect, carpenter, or handyman, was valuable in God's eyes. And that life was more about love and intimacy than random sexual conquests, as wonderful as sex was.

"What do you know about sex?" said Mark one afternoon.

"I wasn't always a monk, you know," said Paul.

"You *dog*!"

The abbot laughed, confessing that although he wasn't a ladies' man, he had dated and fallen in love twice before entering the monastery. "And I still have the normal urges of any human being."

Paul thought it was healthy for them to talk with one another about their respective lives—one as someone looking for a wife, the other as someone who had vowed chastity, but who still wanted to love and be loved. Paul prayed that Mark would deepen his respect for himself, for what he did and who he was. Sometimes he thought Mark's sleeping around masked a sense that he didn't feel worthy of a long-term relationship. Mark had told him as much a few weeks ago when he admitted, "I'm worried that I get my value from whether or not a woman will go out with me." Most of all, Paul hoped he could help Mark see that God loved him.

Mark also had an unnaturally rosy view of monastic life. After a heated argument with one of his girlfriends, Mark said the next morning, "Maybe I should just move in here and not worry about dealing with human beings anymore."

Paul said, "Who do you think lives here?"

The abbot often had to remind people on the outside that the monastery was no paradise.

Describing life at P&J was like describing a good marriage: hard to sum up. It wasn't perfect, but he loved so many things about it—from the first day he entered.

But it could be lonely. Even after years in the monastery, Paul often caught himself musing about what it would be like to be married to one of the two women he had dated in college. The fact that one had just gotten divorced only seemed to make her more "available," though Paul wondered if she ever even thought of him. Although he enjoyed the community, he missed the intimacy that came with what the monks called an "exclusive relationship." Sex he missed a great deal and thought about that daily. His earlier life had taught him about the joys of that part of life.

Even more did he miss having one person on whom he could rely, on whom he could count, and who relied on him and counted on him. His novice director told him that the biggest challenge of religious life lies in knowing that you'll never be the most important person in anyone else's life. Paul knew that and accepted it. But he didn't like it. Sometimes, when he was listening to one of the monks complain about the food for the second time in as many days, he would think, *I gave up a wife for this?*

He would reproach himself for those feelings, and then reproach himself for reproaching himself. In those times he turned to a line he used with the novices, from the Jesuit poet Gerard Manley Hopkins: "My own heart let me have more pity on."

So as much as Paul felt he could help Anne, he was a little worried about finding her attractive. During their first visit he caught himself staring too intently into her blue eyes and enjoying their conversation too much.

The abbot of the Abbey of Saints Philip and James glanced at the watch his parents had given him for his ordination and realized that the Vespers service was about to start. The bell rang, and Paul smiled. He really did enjoy the comforting stability of monastic life. He decided to offer a special prayer for Anne: that God would console her in her grief, and that he, Paul, would be able to help her as best he could.

18

"Dear God," she wrote.

This was Anne's fifth try; several crumpled sheets in the wastebasket testified to this. She rose from the kitchen table and walked to the window. From there she could see into some of her neighbors' houses, where they were finishing up late dinners, washing dishes, or watching television in their bedrooms. Her own house was so quiet now. She never could fathom how one boy could make so much noise, and she had frequently badgered Jeremiah not to slam doors, talk so loudly on the phone, or scream while he and his friends were in the house playing video games, but now she missed the commotion. Although she liked the quiet in the monastery, the quiet in her house was different. One was a presence, the other an absence.

She looked at the picture of Mary and Jesus on the refrigerator door.

I'm not sure if I believe in you anymore, but I want to tell you something anyway. So it's this: I don't understand why you took

Jeremiah away from me. Why you took him away from this world. Why you made him die the way he did. Why he died, and the other boys lived. I didn't want them to die. But I wanted my son to live. I'll never understand that. Never. He was such a beautiful boy. When he was little, he had the sweetest laugh. It was the most beautiful sound that I ever heard. His father used to say that we should bottle his laughter and give it in big doses to people who were sad, because it would cure them. Jeremiah giggled at everything. I couldn't believe how much I loved him when he was born. I just couldn't believe it. It was like there was this secret reserve of love that I had been saving up all those years just for him, and it all came out on the day of his birth.

When he was a toddler, he was incredibly curious. Exploring from the moment he could crawl. Getting into cupboards and trying to open all the closets with his pudgy little hands, because he just had to see what was inside. One time I accidentally left the door to the hall closet open, and he pushed himself up high enough so that he could grab onto a shelf and pull down a whole comforter on top of himself—and he just laughed. And he wasn't afraid at all. Other children would have cried. But he loved it. He loved looking at the world. When people saw him crawling all over the place they would say, "Watch out when he starts walking!" His father gave him a little T-shirt that said, "Here comes trouble!"

But he wasn't a troublemaker at all. He was such a sweet kid. Used to love to watch the ants going into their little holes in the pavement, the birds perching on the bird feeder, and he could spend hours looking for bugs under the rocks in the garden. Liked books too. *All my picture books and atlases from the places Eddie and I had been. "Where's this? Where's this? Where's this?" he'd say. He told me once that the way that he looked at the maps was the way that God looks at us. I can't believe I just remembered that. I bought him a little plastic globe when he was three, and he played with it like other kids play with baseballs. He took it with him everywhere for a few months.*

After his father left us, I worried about his not having a man around, and that I wouldn't be able to handle raising a boy, but I did, and later on I worried about Jeremiah being too shy to have friends. But he was okay. Some of the kids teased him because of his little stutter in kindergarten, but by the second grade that was almost gone and he could fit in. The teachers all loved him, because he was so sweet.

God, I always worried that he would turn into someone I couldn't handle, especially as he got older. That he would surprise me and turn into someone else. That I would lose him. I knew enough sullen teenagers. But he was okay. He was more than okay. All along he was okay. He was a lovely kid. I loved him so much. He wasn't perfect. Who is? I'm not. His father certainly isn't. But Jeremiah was a beautiful boy. Beautiful. Beautiful. Beautiful.

Then when he started to hang around with Brad and the kids from the neighborhood, he really blossomed. Boy, he loved playing with them, and I loved seeing him get dirty and laugh; even when he got hurt, he thought it was okay because he was with them. They didn't seem afraid of anything and he

Anne's chest tightened, and she was tempted to stop writing. But she scratched out "and he," put a period after "anything," and continued.

Maybe they should have been. The night of the accident he begged me to go to that movie. Begged me. Begged me. "Can't you please drive us?" Everyone else's parents were busy. But I didn't want him to see that movie. It was too violent, and it was too late. I need to remember that. The therapist told me that. I was protecting him. I was. I was protecting him because I loved him. I need to remember that I didn't want to drive him and told him to stay home because I loved him.

God, when the police knocked on my door, I knew what it was. I just knew. That knock sounded terrifying. No one else knows that. I knew when I heard the knock. So loud. When I opened the door, I couldn't breathe. I saw the blue uniforms, and I heard their voices, and I just screamed. Sometimes I see that terrible blue color in my nightmares. I feel like I've been screaming ever since.

God, why did you do this? How could you do this to my beautiful boy who loved your world and whom I loved so much? I miss him so much, and I would do anything to see him even one more time. Just so I could say good-bye and hug him and kiss him and let him know how much I love him. And I don't know if there's a heaven, but I want to see him again, and I can't believe I won't see him again, so I guess I believe in heaven now.

Anne set her pen down. Rereading the letter, she was surprised. It wasn't as angry as she thought it would be. It was more sad than angry. It was more about Jeremiah than about God. It was more about telling God about Jeremiah. She wondered if this was what Father Paul had in mind. Maybe it wasn't the way you should write a letter to God. She picked up the paper and hunted around in a dining room cabinet, crammed with bills, for an envelope to put it in. One was at the bottom of the drawer. Folding her letter carefully, she placed it inside the envelope.

She took it out again because she forgot something. At the bottom of the page she wrote:

Anne

Now what?

19

Gardening was one thing that kept Anne sane after the accident. Her full list of sanity-preserving measures would have included: dinners with Kerry, who always made her laugh; yoga classes in Bryn Mawr, which lent her weekends a measure of calm; talking on the phone with her roommate from Haverford; going to work every day, even if she wasn't always crazy about the job; and long walks by the Wissahickon River, especially in the spring and summer.

But gardening she could do without having to leave the house, or at least the yard, which helped when she didn't feel like seeing anyone or driving anywhere. Even when she felt sullen, she could work outside by herself. Plus she liked wearing her mother's straw gardening hat and her father's old canvas gloves, which smelled like years of work, sticking her hands into the moist earth, and feeling like she was doing something.

Today she was planting batches of zinnias, marigolds, pansies, and snapdragons that she bought on sale at the supermarket. The oranges and yellows and pinks and purples looked

132 ❖ JAMES MARTIN, SJ

so glorious on the metal shelves outside the market that she grabbed as many of the green plastic trays as she could and piled them on top of the groceries in her shopping cart.

The potting shed was one of the few things her husband left behind that she used without feeling resentment toward him. Eddie had been her boyfriend since high school, and although she worried about his laziness even then, his near complete lack of drive after he graduated from college stunned her. His job at the insurance agency paid well enough, but he seemed uninterested in even trying to move up through the ranks.

What bothered Anne much more was his lackadaisical care of Jeremiah. She never did figure out if it was inability or unwillingness. Eddie was wildly enthusiastic during the pregnancy, reading books and going online to learn about child care, and helping her as much as any expectant father would. At Jeremiah's birth, Eddie was exultant, spending hours staring at him in his crib, buying him little Eagles and Phillies shirts and bibs, sending photos to his family, and even bringing Jeremiah to work one day to show him off to his friends.

But after a year, when it became clear that parenting wasn't about showing off your baby—that is, when it came to changing diapers, getting up for early-morning feedings, and taking Jeremiah to the pediatrician when he got one of his frequent ear infections—Eddie was largely useless.

"I'm too tired. I just can't do this anymore," he said once during one of Jeremiah's late-night screaming jags.

"You think I'm not tired?" she shouted over the baby's squalling.

Eddie loved Jeremiah. He just didn't want to take care of him.

So she wasn't as shocked as her friends were when he decided to "spend some time apart." Kerry told Anne that if it were her husband, she would have him castrated. "If he had any balls to begin with," said Kerry.

At the time, Anne was so busy caring for Jeremiah, working in the accounting firm, and driving back and forth to day care to have any energy to think about anything other than her child. "I'm too tired to be angry," she told Kerry. If anything, she was disappointed. Sad. But not angry. Not yet at least. The person she thought she had known best proved to be someone who, in the end, she didn't seem to know well at all.

So when he asked for a divorce, she gave it to him. Just like that. The alimony wasn't much—Eddie's spotty job record made that an easy prediction—but it helped, especially when Jeremiah was a toddler. Anne would get angry at Eddie only years later, when the full magnitude of his colossal irresponsibility dawned on her.

When she pulled the marigolds from their plastic tubs, their roots emerged with an audible rip. She knelt on the edge of her backyard garden, pushed aside some warm brown soil with her gloved hand, made a tidy hole, filled it with a handful of fertilizer, poured in a little water, placed a bunch of yellow and orange marigolds into the opening, filled the rest of the hole with soil, and patted it down with a satisfying thump. That was her favorite part of working in the garden—gently tamping down the soil. She always asked her mother, the gardener in the family, if she could do that during her mother's yearly plantings. It felt like she was protecting the flowers.

She watered the flowers at their base, and sprinkled a little on the petals, knowing not to overdo it during the daytime. Her mother had told her many times that too much water could burn the petals and leaves if the sun was strong. "You want to water them, not bake them," she said. Anne remembered the feel of her mother's hand steadying her own, helping her hold the same battered metal watering can that Anne used now. How old was she then? Eight? Nine?

A small worm, unearthed by her plantings, writhed on the top of a mound of dirt—helpless, confused, unseeing. Anne's felt sorry for the worm, who twisted and spun. Gently, she moved him out of reach of her trowel. She wondered if it would be better to bury him under a handful of soil or leave him to find his way back into the earth. She left him. An unseen robin sang from a bough in a pine tree in her neighbor's yard.

For sheer pleasure, she took off her father's gloves and plunged her hands, almost up to the wrists, as far as they could go, into the loose dark soil to feel the warm earth.

Anne planted the zinnias and pansies next, leaving the snapdragons, her favorites, for last. When she was a girl, riding her bike to elementary school, she would often pause in a meadow just outside the school grounds and watch the wild snapdragons loll in the wind, their bright yellow and dusty lavender heads bobbing in the sun. It was this memory that came to her now. She wondered, all of a sudden, if Jeremiah had inherited his love of nature from her. Why hadn't she thought of that before?

Still kneeling, she raised her head, at eye level with the taller blossoms. The orange and red zinnias she had planted last week had taken root. Now they were almost as high as the new pink snapdragons. And beneath them, the yellow and orange marigolds took up almost every inch of the garden. Suddenly Anne had an unfamiliar appreciation of beauty. The vivid color of the flowers in the bright May sunlight was like a scene from a postcard. Anne could hear the faint drone of a lawnmower, borne on the wind, but other than that, there was only silence.

Then she had a strange feeling—almost as if God was patting down the soil around her life. She felt comforted. Calm.

She looked up, as if expecting someone to say something. But there was only the wind.

That was odd. As she watered the newly planted flowers, Anne felt a desire to ask Father Paul about those feelings. Then she rolled her eyes. *If you had told me a few months ago that I would be thinking about a monastery when I was planting flowers...*

"Hey!" a man's voice said behind her.

Still kneeling, Anne turned and saw Mark's legs, tanned and sweaty. He was wearing nylon shorts, beat-up sneakers, and a faded Red Sox T-shirt, apparently having finished a run. Kerry once had told her how attractive she thought Mark was, and now Anne had to agree. A few years ago she might have pursued him, but she was dissuaded by their age difference. Kerry disagreed. "Go for it."

"Need any help?" he asked.

"No thanks," she said. "But it's nice of you to ask. I'm pretty much done." She stood up, clapped the dirt from her hands, and brushed some loose soil off her shorts.

"Garden looks nice. Hey, how's that car?" he said.

"Crappy," she said, smiling. "But it works."

"That's cool." She could tell by his look—that swift visual assessment of her face, legs, and whatever else, which some men were so expert at doing without being obvious or rude—that he appreciated whatever he saw in her this morning.

"By the way," she said, "I stopped by that monastery of yours again the other day."

"Really? How come?"

"You remember the monk my dad knew, Father Edward? Well, I wanted to visit him again. I thought he could use the company."

"That's nice of you. Did you have a good talk with him? He's a lot of fun, isn't he?"

"No, he was sick, so I couldn't see him."

"Oh yeah, that's right." said Mark. "Father Paul told me he wasn't feeling well."

"So I spoke to Father Paul instead," she said. He looked a bit surprised at that, so she followed quickly with, "You know, you *could* help me with this bag of fertilizer. I pulled a muscle in yoga the other day, and I can't really lift it."

"That's ironic," he said. "Isn't yoga supposed to make you flexible?"

"It does," she said. "But, you know, sometimes you overdo it."

Mark hoisted the heavy bag with one hand. *Show off,* she thought and turned her back to lead him to the potting shed. He was likeable enough, and she sensed his interest, but what a frat boy. She had had enough of that for one lifetime.

Somehow he arrived at the shed before she did. Reaching around his sweaty T-shirt, she opened the shed door. "Just stick it on the ledge," she said.

"Hey, um," he said after emerging from the shed into the sunshine, "would you maybe want to go out for a drink sometime?"

Frat boy or not, it was still nice to get compliments. "Oh, I don't go out with tenants."

His face fell for just an instant and then, recovering, he grinned again, falsely. "Oh, um, I didn't mean on a date, you know, I meant more like . . ."

"Oh, I know," she said. "I was just teasing." She turned and began walking back to the garden, to spare him the indignity of her witnessing his disappointment. "Maybe sometime we could get a drink, but I'm pretty busy these days. But thanks."

"That's cool. Need any more help right now?"

"No, but thanks. Big help already."

Mark raised his eyebrows, smiled, and raised his hand in a farewell. Then he walked quickly into her front yard and onto the sidewalk, where he continued his jog back to his house.

Well, that was awkward. Anne thought about how much she missed sex, how she used to enjoy it with Eddie in the early mornings during the first few months of their marriage. She wiped the sweat from her forehead and then gathered up her gardening tools.

But those flowers. And that odd feeling of comfort. Maybe it wouldn't hurt to talk to Father Paul again.

20

Later that day, Anne called the guest house, talked to Maddy, and made an appointment to see Paul. Maddy told her that Father Edward was feeling better, but was still not taking visitors. "Abbot's orders."

On Monday she brought the jam to Kerry's office and placed the jar on her desk with a thump.

"Yum," Kerry said. "And thanks. The blueberry is my all-time favorite. My mom used to make these amazing peanut butter and blueberry jam sandwiches for us and pack them in our lunch bags for school. We even brought those jars to the shore. Those monks make some kickass jam. How was your trip there? Did they convert you?"

Anne laughed. "Well, I'm Catholic already, so there wouldn't have been much use in that."

Later on, over sandwiches and sodas in the small employee lunchroom—an unused office with four tables, a mini refrigerator, and an unreliable coffee machine—Anne told Kerry about her time with Father Paul and how kind he was to her. She couldn't *not* tell Kerry, but also worried about her response. Kerry had just disagreed with the way Anne handled Mark after she told her about their time by the potting shed. "He's hot," she said. "You should have at least agreed to a drink!"

Anne explained how she had gone to visit Father Edward and ended up speaking to the abbot. But she didn't tell her about the letter he asked her to write.

"The abbot?" she said. "Is that what their leader is called? I guess that makes sense. It's an abbey, right? Is it like the mother abbess in *The Sound of Music*? Is he like a male mother abbess? Does he sing? Did he tell you to climb every mountain?"

Anne laughed again. "I think *she's* probably like a female abbot. I guess. They sing there, but it's not Rogers and Hammerstein. It's all Gregorian chant."

"Well, that's cool," said Kerry. "I'm glad he was nice to you. You deserve it. The ministers I knew growing up were okay. Most of them. Did I ever tell you about all those Presbyterian youth groups my parents made me go to? They were pretty fun. Roller skating. Ice skating. Presbyterians skate a lot, apparently. Plus, ice cream. We were always eating ice cream. One weekend we all went to some retreat house in the sticks somewhere in the Poconos and played games and talked about Jesus. And had ice cream, of course. It was pretty fun, actually. But church isn't my style anymore. I'm glad he's nice to you, though. What's he like?"

"Father Paul?" said Anne, taking a sip of her Diet Coke.

"Um, well, you know. He's a priest, or a monk, so . . . I don't know. He's nice. He listens. I actually, um . . ."

"You . . . what?"

"I kind of like going there. It's peaceful, you know? And pretty. And there are worse things in the world than peaceful and pretty."

"True," said Kerry. "Just be careful. You don't want to turn into some sort of religious fanatic."

Anne put down the soda can and raised her right hand. "I vow that I will not become a religious fanatic. So help me God."

21

"I'm not sure what to do with this," said Anne as she reached across the coffee table and handed Father Paul a white envelope.

The two were in the abbot's office after Vespers. The waning sunlight filtered through the leaves of the maple tree outside Paul's window, dappling the faded oriental carpet and the red wingback chairs on which they sat. A few minutes ago at the guest house, Maddy had surprised Anne by greeting her with a hug and then led her to the abbot's office.

Paul examined the blank envelope. No address and no return address.

"I'm sorry," he said. "Who's this for?"

"It's the letter to God," said Anne. "Remember?"

"Ah yes. Of course," said Paul. "What was it like writing it?"

"Well, it felt good to get my thoughts down on paper," said Anne. "Actually, I thought I was going to be angrier, but I wasn't. I don't know why, but I wasn't. It was more sad than angry. And more of it turned out to be about Jeremiah than about God." Anne paused. "Do you want to read it?"

"No," said Paul, smiling. "Thank you." He handed the envelope back to her and then smoothed the front of the black scapular that covered his white robe. "It's a letter to God, not to me. I'm glad you wrote it. And I'm sure God has already heard what you have to say."

"Well," she said, "I hope so. Sometimes I'm not sure about all that. Sometimes I think that even if God does exist, I'm not sure I want to know him."

Paul's gaze seemed to invite her to continue.

"I mean, sometimes I think I'd *like* to believe in God," she said. "And I think about how much my parents believed, and what a comfort it was to them. But then I think about the way that God *is*. He took away my son, first of all, so why would I want to believe in a God like that? It seems so . . . masochistic."

The abbot's face revealed neither surprise nor disapproval.

"Plus," she continued, "I keep thinking about this person in the sky who's judging me every minute of the day. Looking at everything I do—all the times I didn't go to Mass, all the times I got angry after Jeremiah's death, and all the times that I got pissed off at my ex-husband—and ticking off everything in little boxes that say 'Right' and 'Wrong.' Then when I come to the end of my life, there will be too many checks in the 'Wrong' box, and I'll go to hell. When I was little, my parents used to say, 'We may not be able to see everything you do, but *God* does.' It used to freak me out. So who wants to believe in a God like that? Not me."

"Me neither," said Paul. "That's not the God I believe in."

Anne squinted in confusion.

"Look, I do believe God will judge us at the end of our lives. Jesus tells us that in the Gospels. And, at least as I see it, a God who didn't judge what we do is a God who doesn't care how we live. And who would want to believe in a God who doesn't care how we treat each other? But for me God is much more about mercy and love than about judgment and punishment. We see that over and over in Jesus's parables. Can I ask you a question?"

Anne nodded.

"Are there any similarities between the way you viewed your parents and the way you view God?"

Anne considered that for a moment.

"Sometimes," Paul continued, "our images of God come from the way our parents treated us. So if we had parents who were judgmental or harsh or exacting, we often transfer those same attributes to God. This ends up influencing the way we relate to God. That's why I'm asking."

Anne looked out the window and strained to see the sunset through the leaves. "I'm embarrassed to say this, because I loved both of my parents and they were really wonderful people, but . . ."

"That's okay," said Paul. "I'm not saying this to denigrate your parents, but to invite you to understand your relationship to God better."

"I have to admit," she said, clearing her throat, "that my parents, loving as they were, were pretty, um, demanding."

"In what way?"

"Well," she said, shifting in her seat, "I had to sign a little sheet every night that was posted on the refrigerator that said that I did my chores for the day, and I had to make sure all my toys were always put away in my room or my mom would freak out, and I had to bring my homework to my dad every night for him to review. And if I didn't do those things, there was hell to pay."

"Really?" said Paul. "Hell to pay? That's an interesting choice of words."

"What are you getting at?"

"God is not your parents," he said. "Just because your parents were demanding doesn't mean that God is like that. Sometimes we have an image of God that really isn't God. And we get stuck on that God. It's *Anne's* God that you're talking about. It's Anne's God who is the harsh taskmaster. It's Anne's God you don't want to relate to."

"I'm not sure I follow."

"I'm talking about your images of God," said Paul, "and how they influence the way you relate to God. Are there any other images of God that you like?"

All at once Anne remembered her experience in the garden. How peculiar. She had come here planning to tell Paul about it, and then forgot, and was now happy to have remembered. It was the reason she was here. "Actually, the weirdest thing happened the other day," she said.

Paul held out his right hand, palm up, by way of encouragement.

"So I'm in the yard the other day, gardening. Which I

really like to do. It was on Sunday. Remember how nice it was Sunday?"

Paul nodded.

She told the story—of working with the plants, patting down the soil, remembering her mother, the strange recognition, the unfamiliar sense of God.

"I thought," she said, "that it felt like God was patting down the soil . . . around me, sort of."

A gentle smile came to Paul's face.

"Does that sound insane?"

"Not at all. It sounds beautiful. God is the gardener who tends you like a flower, who nourishes you, just as you care for the plants in your own garden. That's lovely. It's also wonderful that you connected that to a comforting image of your mother. Can you let that be your image of God for now?"

"What do you mean?"

"Well," he said, "that image may be a gift from God. It may be a way that God's inviting you to see things in a new light. Who says that you have to think of God only as a judge? Who says that's the only image you can use? There are lots of images of God. And I think God's just given you a new one."

Anne looked at him, drinking in his words.

"Funny enough," said Paul, "that's a common image in the spiritual life. You know, after Jesus rises from the dead on Easter and appears to Mary Magdalene, she thinks he's the gardener."

"Yeah," said Anne. "I remember that story. Always seemed hard to understand."

"It *is* a little mysterious. It's strange that Mary can't recognize him after the Resurrection. After all, it wasn't like she had never seen him before. But maybe the way he looked after the Resurrection was a little . . . different. In any event, she thinks he's the gardener until he says her name. Since then there's been a tradition in painting of portraying Jesus as a gardener. So you'll even see paintings of Jesus appearing to Mary with some gardening tools. It's really quite beautiful."

Anne could feel something within her relaxing, settling into the sound of Paul's voice. She wanted to hear more and was happy when he continued.

"And there are all sorts of wonderful ways of thinking about that. I mean, from a spiritual point of view. One of the old monks here likes to say that God plows up our soul and moves things around—as you do in a garden—so that new things can be planted there. You know how you pull up rocks and weeds to make room for new plantings in the spring? God shakes things up a bit in our lives, and it's hard and painful sometimes, but all that earth moving can allow for something new to take root and bloom."

That image appealed to Anne, and she smiled.

Paul asked, "Do you know about St. Thérèse of Lisieux?"

"I'm really not up on my saints."

"Well, she's often called the Little Flower and—"

"Oh," said Anne. "The Little Flower? Oh, I remember her. My parents had a picture of her in their bedroom. I don't know much about her, though. What's her story?"

"Well, Thérèse of Lisieux was a Carmelite nun in the late nineteenth century in a little town in France, called—needless to say—Lisieux. She lost her mother when she was very young, maybe three or four, was adored by her father, and was pretty spoiled by her sisters. She lived in a cloistered monastery, so you'd figure that no one would know about her once she had entered the monastery. But she wrote this wonderful autobiography, and it's just magnificent. Anyway, there is a passage about the way God looks at us, sort of like we're God's garden, and it . . . wait a minute."

Paul went to his bookcase and pulled out a dog-eared gray paperback. He flipped through the pages. "Here it is."

He sat down and read a passage that Anne could see was underlined in blue ink:

> I understood how all the flowers God has created are beautiful, how the splendor of the rose and the whiteness of the lily do not take away the perfume of the little violet or the delightful simplicity of the daisy. I understood that if all flowers wanted to be roses, nature would lose her springtime beauty, and the fields would no longer be decked out with little wildflowers. And so it is in the world of souls, Jesus' garden. . . . He has created smaller ones and these must be content to be daisies or violets destined to give joy to God's glances when He looks down at His feet. Perfection consists in doing His will, in being what He wills us to be.

"That's pretty," said Anne.

"So the image of you in God's garden is in line with some

of the saints' images. But here's the point, Anne: it's an image that God gave *you*. Think about this: where do you think the image came from?"

"I don't know. From my imagination?"

"That's true. But you could also say that God planted that seed in your imagination, ready to flower when you were ready. That's the way God communicates with us—in very personal ways."

Anne sat back in her chair. The idea that God was something, or someone, or whatever, who would communicate with her was new. And confusing. "That's a lot to take in."

Paul waited.

"But it's nice."

"God wants to be in relationship with us," said Paul. "And God wants to be in relationship with *you*. And the first step in that relationship is trusting that this is true. Like in any relationship. It also means recognizing that these kinds of experiences are God's way of starting the conversation. And does that sound like a judging God?"

"No, actually," she said, "it doesn't."

"In fact," he said, "if you think about the images of God that Jesus uses in the Gospels, it's a lot more than simply a God who judges. Certainly Jesus talks about the Last Judgment, but there's a lot more about a merciful and compassionate God."

"For example?"

"Well, like the story of the prodigal son, where the son runs away from home, spends all his inheritance, and then comes back home again. Most people know that the father welcomes him back. But what they sometimes forget is that the son hasn't even apologized yet. I mean, in the story the son decides to apologize, but the father rushes out to welcome him before the son says a word. That's one of my favorite images of God. He judges—sure, the father doesn't approve of what the son did—but most of all the father welcomes, he forgives, and he loves."

Anne stared at him.

"Or think about the woman who lost her coin. Do you know that one?"

"Sorry, I'm really striking out here."

"That's okay," he said. "It's not as well known. Jesus said that God is like the woman who loses a coin and sweeps her whole house to find it. That's how much God wants to find us. It's something like the parable of the lost sheep too, where God is like the shepherd who leaves the whole flock behind to find the one lost sheep. They're both images of God constantly searching for us. And that's the God who is inviting you right now, into . . ."

"Into what?"

"Into a relationship."

Anne leaned back in the chair and looked out the window at the pink and orange clouds. She felt a strange mix of fear, curiosity, and elation. But mainly curiosity. Because she couldn't deny what she had experienced in the garden. It happened. And she couldn't deny that Father Paul's words were appealing. They were. She liked those images of God too. But the idea of God communicating with her seemed weird. And somewhat frightening. Anne didn't want to become some sort of religious freak and tell people that God was talking to her.

"Okay," she said. "I'll bite. So what am I supposed to do?"

"Why not just let God be God and continue to speak to you in whatever way God wants. And let it be God, not Anne's God, not your old images of God, but *God*. And maybe you'd like to say something back to that God." He smiled. "Maybe you'd like to give him that letter."

The monastery bell tolled.

"After Compline," he said, standing up and smoothing his habit. "I'll be right back. Unless you'd like to join us?"

"Not yet," she said. "I mean, um, no thanks."

22

During Compline, Anne sat in Father Paul's office, watching the orange sunset through the dark leaves of the maple tree and listening to the chants echo through the halls of the abbey. She anticipated the chanting of the Salve Regina. When the monks started to sing her father's song, she rose from her chair and walked out into the hallway to hear it more clearly. As she leaned against the cold brick wall, she felt a kind of support. A holding. Then the great bell rang again, signaling the end of the prayer. When she heard the monks leaving their seats in the chapel, she ducked back inside the office.

As the monks glided past the abbot's office, a few absentmindedly peered in and then, noticing her, abruptly turned their faces back to the tiled floor.

Father Edward shuffled by, gripping a metal walker, and glanced into the office. "Annie!" he said with a smile. "Oh, I was so sorry I missed you the other day! I'm so happy to see you. I've been praying for you."

The way his words tumbled out touched Anne. The only other person who greeted her so cheerfully was Sunshine, who wasn't even a person. And that was only at mealtimes.

Laboriously, Father Edward moved his bulk into the abbot's office. Anne awkwardly leaned over his walker, which had rosary beads twined around one of the handles, and kissed the old monk on his rough cheek. He blushed.

"Oh, it's such a blessing to see you," he said again. "Are you meeting with Father Abbot?"

"Well, yes," she said. "I wanted to stop by tonight and see you as well. Are you feeling better?"

"Oh yes, yes. Just a little bronchitis, thank God. It takes me a little longer to recover these days."

When the abbot walked in, Father Edward started to push himself up to a standing position.

"Oh, Father," said Paul. "Please don't get up. Save your strength."

Anne suddenly felt uncomfortable. *How have I come to this, sitting with two monks in a monastery?* She imagined Kerry teasing her about this tableau. A faint smile came to her lips, but she willed it away. Then she thought about her father and how happy he would be to see her here.

"Do you think you might visit with me after you're finished speaking with Father Abbot?"

"I'd be happy to," she said.

"Do I have your permission?" he asked the abbot.

"Of course," said Paul.

Father Edward shuffled out of the office.

After he was out of earshot, Anne asked, "Is he really okay?"

"Yes, I'm happy to say that he is," said Paul. "He's dying of course, but—"

Anne's eyes widened. "*What?*"

"Sorry," he said. "It's what we sometimes say here. I mean that we're *all* dying. All of us are moving toward death. But yes, Father Edward is doing fine. Just the normal aches and pains of human life. One of our abbots used to say that, rather than looking at our bodies as something permanent and getting upset when things break down, it makes more sense to see our bodies as something impermanent and bound to break down. The same way that you don't expect a pair of pants to last forever, you shouldn't expect your body to do the same. In the end, they both have wrinkles and holes and start to fall apart. So when things start to decline, it's not as frightening. It's to be expected."

"That doesn't make getting older any easier," said Anne.

"No, not easier. But it makes it more . . . expected. Somehow that's always helped me," he said with a shrug.

Anne didn't want to get drawn into a discussion about aging, and she still wanted to visit Father Edward and get home before it was too late, so she got to her point.

"So how do you propose I deliver my letter to God? Or maybe I should call. Do you have a direct line here?"

Paul revealed a gap-toothed smile. "Oh, that's pretty good! No, we don't have a direct line. But maybe you could say that it's a local call. God's already heard you, of course, but why don't we place your letter before the image of Our Lady that you like? There's a little basket for petitions that visitors often use. How does that sound? You can do that after you visit Father Edward."

The old priest was bunking temporarily in the infirmary, and as Anne was escorted there by Father Paul, she noticed parts of the abbey that she had overlooked before. Familiarity gave her new eyes.

She liked the orderliness most of all. Everything seemed to be in its place, nothing like her home—where boxes and books and clothes and papers and files were scattered everywhere. Here all the white cowls were on their pegs, all the gray pots on their hooks in the kitchen, and all the red prayer books lined up on their shelves. The simplicity of the building itself also appealed to her. It was big, no doubt, but somehow the architecture, with its clean lines and almost total lack of ornamentation, mirrored the austerity of the men who lived here. The monks walked close to the brick walls as they passed her rather than in the middle of the hallway, as if reverencing the spaces in the wide hallways and making room for one another. She liked how the cloister garden looked at dusk, with the slim branches of the dogwood and cherry trees swaying gently in the summer breeze.

An understanding of why her father liked coming here deepened in her. Quite unexpectedly, she felt an intense burst of love for him.

Father Edward's infirmary room was sparely furnished: a metal hospital bed, a small porcelain sink, an old easy chair in which he now sat, and an ancient wooden desk, nicked in places. A gathering of squat plastic pill bottles stood grimly on a nightstand beside a framed portrait of a female saint wearing a brown-and-white nun's habit and holding a bouquet of roses. As Father Paul sat on Father Edward's bed and Anne on a rickety wooden desk chair, the old monk began talking about her parents.

Her father began coming here after attending a men's weekend retreat that his parish had sponsored. On the last day of the retreat the abbot asked if any of the men present had any accounting experience and if anyone would like to help the monastery out of a tough spot. Father Edward said her father's expertise saved the monastery at a difficult time. The previous accountant was not exactly "unscrupulous" (Anne hadn't heard that word for a while), but he was "unhelpful." Apparently, not only did the former accountant occasionally clash with the abbot; he also couldn't be counted on to pay the abbey's bills on time. Anne's father, by contrast, was "a boon" to them and ended up being devoted to the monks. "It was a great relief to the abbot when he came. It meant that he could relax more about the finances and concentrate on other things."

Anne's mother too attended women's retreats at the abbey, something Anne was surprised to learn. Father Edward said he didn't know why she stopped coming, but by calculating backward from the dates that the old priest mentioned, Anne figured that her own birth had afforded her mother less free time.

Hearing about her parent's piety and their relationship to the abbey was both comforting and unsettling. It was odd to hear stories about her mother and father from this elderly monk, who in some ways seemed to know them better than she did. And it was strange to think of her parents as not only religious in the sense of following a set of rules, but religious in the sense of what Anne was beginning to understand about prayer. Her parents, whose spirituality she had dismissed as superficial and at times naive, were starting to seem, in a way, more sophisticated than she was.

"Oh, and look," Father Edward said. He took a Bible from his nightstand and gingerly pulled out an old photo from between its thin pages. "Look who I found!"

With a slightly shaking hand, he gave Anne a faded photo of her mother in a flowered pink dress, her father in a brown suit, and a much younger Father Edward, in a white alb and golden stole, pouring water over a baby's head in a church.

"That's you."

Anne looked carefully at her baptism. She had never seen this photo before. Her parents weren't much for photo albums or home movies. Anne's mother kept a leather wedding album and a few other family pictures in a shoebox under her bed. After her mother's death Anne reproached herself for not being able to locate the box; later, in the rush of selling her parents' house, she simply gave up looking. She wondered if she had carelessly thrown it out with whatever else she had considered trash.

"The abbot at the time gave me special permission to leave

the monastery to do your baptism. All because of our gratitude to your father. Look how little you were, Annie," he said,
pointing his gnarled finger to the baby nestled in her mother's
arms. "They were so happy that day." Anne felt her throat
tighten.

"I was proud to welcome you into the church," he said.

With some formality, he handed Anne the photo and then
asked if he could bless her. She looked at Paul, who wordlessly
met her gaze.

When Paul nodded, Father Edward motioned for her to
come closer. She stood and moved beside the easy chair, not
knowing what to do, and he chuckled.

"Come closer, dear."

When she bent down, he grasped her head with his shaking
hands and was silent. Then he whispered, "Amen."

After saying their good-byes, Father Paul led Anne to the
abbey church. "Stay as long as you like," he said. "And come
back whenever you like." Then Father Paul left her.

By now the church was almost completely dark, except
for the light coming from a bronze lamp hanging near the
altar. The blue stained-glass windows let in only the slightest
amount of light, so that even during the daytime the space
was largely held in shadow. Anne walked up to the heavy
wooden table that supported the image of Mary, who seemed
to fix her gaze on Anne.

Now Mary's expression seemed more compassionate. It was
strange how the same image could look so different after you
came to know it.

On the table, underneath the painting, sat a round wicker basket in which dozens of letters were stuffed. Most were concealed in envelopes, but many were written on loose pieces of paper. She couldn't help reading some:

Mary, pray that my father's cancer will be cured.

Let me have a child, God.

Please, God, if it is your will, help me to find a job.

God, I pray not to be so lonely.

Thank you for your prayers, Mary.

Anne wasn't sure how she felt about the requests. On the one hand, they touched her. On the other, they seemed superstitious. Why would you ask Mary for her prayers if you could just ask God for something? It seemed like an unnecessary step.

Anne wondered whether it made sense to put a letter to God in a box in front of a picture of Mary. Then she looked at Mary's face and decided that this was as good a place as any. She stuffed the letter in among the other petitions, stepped back a few feet, and then said, silently, "Well, Mary, if you're there, please give this letter to God." She was glad she didn't say it out loud, because she thought it would have sounded embarrassing. But silently it felt okay.

Seeing no one else around, she sat in one of the pews in the visitors' section. She would have preferred to sit closer, in the monks' stalls, nearer to the image of Mary, or even on the tile floor, but she worried about what would happen if someone noticed her. The old pew creaked as it accepted her body, and then the chapel was silent. Crickets chorused outside. For the first time since Jeremiah died, Anne tried to formulate a prayer. Despite herself, she repeated the title of a book she had read in junior high school. She couldn't figure out how else to begin.

"Are you there, God?" she said silently. "It's me, Annie."

23

Mark looked at the vast lawn and groaned. Was it possible that the abbey's property had grown larger since the last time he mowed it? It seemed that way. After a lawn-mowing day, which came twice a month, Mark would drive home, take a shower, go for a run, and then take a second shower just to wash all the grassy smell from his body. Even then, when he closed his eyes at night, all he saw was green and all he smelled was grass.

Today, under a sweat-stained Red Sox cap, he cursed himself for making a pass at Anne over the weekend. "Shit!" he shouted over the noise of the abbey's colossal riding lawn-mower. Because who could hear him? Sometimes he felt as if his libido overpowered him. Even worse, he felt embarrassed when rebuffed by a woman: foolish, embarrassed, and diminished in his own eyes. "Unmanned" was a word he recently read in a biography that he didn't finish. He didn't know precisely what it meant and was too tired to look it up in a dictionary, but he had a definite feeling about the word, and that's how he felt.

It had been that way since junior high. When a woman responded to his advances and they ended up making out or dating, he felt good about himself, and those positive vibes colored all he did: his work, his interactions with his friends, even his running. He felt as though he ran faster when his romantic life was where he wanted it to be.

Mark made a sweeping turn on the green-and-yellow lawnmower and from the valley contemplated the view of the abbey church on the crest of the hill. The days when Mark was angry or frustrated—as today, thanks to his interaction with Anne—were good ones for doing physical labor.

Working with his hands often helped get his mind off of his mind. Until he began architecture school, Mark always had a job that required physical activity. As a teenager he mowed lawns and even started a small yard-work business with three of his high-school friends. As the lawnmower rumbled beneath him, he thought of how many of his neighbors' lawns he could have mowed with this monster.

In college, at Northeastern, while trying to decide on a major, he stumbled on a job with a middle-aged carpenter in Cambridge. Mike, a friend of his father's, ran a flourishing business fixing up old houses in tony towns on Cape Cod and in wealthy South Shore towns like Hingham and Cohasset. At the beginning of his apprenticeship Mark was allowed to do only simple tasks, like measuring and sanding, but by the summer of his junior year in college he was entrusted with something that gave him great pride: building, on his own, three matching bookcases for a library in an elegant home being renovated on the Cape. The owners, an elderly couple who had both taught at Harvard, said that it was their favorite part of their home.

One night Mark told his parents how proud he was that he had built them on his own, and his father praised him, but reminded him, gently, "Mike taught you, didn't he?"

Mark started up the hill, the trickiest part of mowing the abbey lawn. Occasionally he worried about the mower flipping over, though it never had, and Brother Robert told him that if Brother Thomas could mow the lawn, then so could Mark. Apparently, Brother Thomas was pretty hopeless with machines. Ten years ago, he totaled two of the monastery's cars before the abbot at the time made him promise that he would always ask someone else to drive him. "Is this a vow?" asked Brother Thomas. "As far as I'm concerned it is," said the abbot.

As he looked at the storage shed, which needed a paint job, Mark thought about how little carpentry work he had done at the monastery. Early in his stay, he built two pine shelves for the jam factory's storage facility, but since then hadn't been called upon to do much else. And for the past few weeks he seemed to have done nothing but paint and plaster. Did the builders construct the abbey so that it would spring leaks every few weeks? For a solid-looking building, it wasn't sturdy at all. "The original builders had to cut some corners," Father Paul admitted once. "Donations weren't as robust as what the archbishop had anticipated."

Mark grew frustrated that his hopes to do more carpentry at the abbey had largely come to naught. He briefly closed his eyes when he recalled his dream, which seemed stupid now, that he would become a renowned local carpenter whose work everyone would flock to see at the abbey. *The famous abbey carpenter,* he thought, and grimaced.

As he bumped over the ground, Mark struggled with a persistent demon: thinking about his friend Dave's life. Married to a wonderful woman, with a good job in Philly and a second child on the way, Dave seemed to have all that Mark wanted, and Mark was ashamed to realize that he was envious. He hated that feeling. Yet he didn't seem to be able to help himself. If only he had taken a different job out of school. If only he had listened to people at the firm who told him not to shoot his mouth off. If only he had kept up with his long-term girlfriend and wasn't such a partier, which she repeatedly told him she hated. If only . . . If only . . .

Father Paul once told him to avoid the *if onlys* and *what ifs.* "They both go nowhere," he said. It was still hard for Mark to avoid going nowhere though, and it bothered him that he was bothered.

Mark maneuvered the lawnmower to the top of the hill, near the abbey church and guest house, when he heard it loudly grind some gravel from the parking lot that found its way into the grass. A loud *ping* rang out as the lawnmower's blades shot a stone into the side of a car parked in the lot.

"Goddammit!" he shouted. He shook his head in disgust, hoping no one had seen it.

"Nice shot!" shouted Father Paul, from under the church portico.

Great. Mark turned off the engine. The big mower slowed to a rumble and was then silent. He climbed down.

"How's the director of the physical plant today?" asked Father Paul, as he strode across the lawn. Grass clippings clung to the bottom of his black-and-white Trappist habit.

"Shitty," Mark said.

Paul's pursed his lips, which Mark took as disapproval of his language.

"What's going on?" asked the abbot.

"Oh, just a lot of bullshit. You know, I don't know what the hell I'm doing here sometimes."

"Well, right now, I think you're mowing the lawn."

Mark didn't know if that was supposed to be funny or profound. It struck him as neither. And it only made him angrier.

"Oh, Christ," he sighed.

"You know," said Paul, frowning. "I'm not a big fan of language like that . . ."

Mark's face fell. "Yes, I know. I'm sorry. I, um . . ."

"What's going on?"

Mark took a deep breath and tried to remind himself that Paul usually gave good advice. "How long do you have?"

"I've got a meeting at the jam factory in a few minutes, but until then I'm all yours."

"I did something stupid," he said, closing his eyes and shaking his head. "The other day I made a pass at someone, and she turned me down. I don't know why, but it makes me really pissed off, and frankly it makes me question what I'm doing with my life."

"That's a big leap—going from one woman not responding to you to questioning your whole life."

Mark looked past Paul's shoulder and into a dark mass of pine trees. "Yeah, I know. It's not that. Well, it is. I don't know. I guess I'm not sure how I got to where I am."

Mark wondered if he should share all this with Paul, and then realized that he couldn't keep it in and that he might not get another chance. He couldn't talk about this with Dave.

"I mean, I've got an architectural degree, and I'm really grateful for the job here, Father Paul, don't get me wrong, and I'm sorry for that language, but I wish I were more settled, and more, well, wealthy or however you want to say it, and I really want to be married to a woman I love. I know you'll tell me that that's greedy or something. Is that wrong to want that?"

"No," said Paul. "It's very right. I'm glad you like it here. You're good at what you do, you know. We're grateful for your presence. But it's okay to want something else."

"I know this will sound strange and, you know, maybe it's the thing with . . ." He started to say her name, but decided against it. "With this woman who's got me down . . . but I feel like I'm, I don't know, sort of embarrassed by what I'm doing here. You know? I get frustrated when that kind of stuff happens, and it ends up confusing me about other things. I have these other friends, and things are going really great for them, like this one friend, and here I am . . ."

Mark looked at the grass. Suddenly he found his throat constricting with emotion, and tears begin to fill his eyes, which surprised him, but mostly made him even angrier.

"Here I am mowing lawns. It's like this job is just . . . a handyman, and I wonder if I'm . . ."

"If you're what?"

"I wonder if I'm going to be stuck here mowing lawns and being a goddamn *handyman* my whole life. Frankly, I don't even know what I feel right now. I'm just pissed off. Everything seems to suck right now."

"Do you mind some advice?"

"Go ahead."

"Well, first try to separate the strands of what's bothering you and not jumble it all together," said Paul. "Just because a relationship with this woman didn't pan out doesn't mean that your whole life is a mess. You might try to avoid using such universal terms, such as 'Everything sucks.'"

"I know," said Mark, looking down at the grass clippings on his beat-up sneakers. Seeing his old shoes suddenly made him feel poor. And embarrassed. "You've told me that before, and I try not to do that. I think I'm more upset about my job. It doesn't feel like I'm where I should be. Sometimes it feels . . ." Mark wiped the sweat from his face with the sleeve of his faded T-shirt. As he did that he also wiped the tears from his eyes, which he didn't want Paul to see.

"It feels . . . beneath me." Mark was embarrassed even as he said it.

"I know I've told you that Jesus was a carpenter, but did I ever talk about the other stuff that Jesus probably did? The word that the Gospel writers used for Jesus's occupation is *tekton*."

"I'm sorry, what?" said Mark, looking directly at Paul. Was he going to get a sermon now?

"*Tekton,*" said Paul. "That's the Greek word that the Gospels use for Jesus's occupation. Most people think that Jesus was a carpenter, but a lot of scholars say that word means not just carpenter, but woodworker, or craftsman, or handyman, or construction worker, or even day laborer. Jesus would have done a lot more than just building doors and tables. He probably helped to build houses and stone walls and all that." Paul smiled. "If he were on earth today, he might even be driving a lawnmower."

"If I were Jesus I'd snap my fingers, and this lawn would be mowed."

"Maybe you would. But maybe you wouldn't. Jesus really worked. I mean, when he was in Nazareth he didn't just snap his fingers and make a table. He built it. The people around him in Nazareth knew him mostly not as a miracle worker, but as a carpenter. I'll bet he was pretty good at what he did too. And I doubt that he had much choice about it. St. Joseph already had a carpentry business, so Jesus probably had go into the family business and follow in Joseph's footsteps. But you have a choice, Mark."

"I know," said Mark, who kicked a stone off the lawn, away from the path of the mower. "I just don't seem to be making the right ones."

"So what's your choice?"

"What do you mean?"

"I mean what do you really want to do in life?"

Mark took in a long breath and let it out. He briefly looked at Paul, and then he looked at the clean lines of the abbey church and the way it sat perfectly on top of the hill, as if the place was made for the building and the building made for the place. He remembered reading that Frank Lloyd Wright was insistent, almost obsessively insistent, that a building appear as if it grew from the surrounding countryside. He looked at the church's red wooden door and the pine benches that sat on the portico under the stone arches. Then he remembered those bookcases on the Cape.

"If I could be a good carpenter," he said, "I would be one."

"Why?"

"When I was in school, what I enjoyed most was making all those little models, which everyone else seemed to hate. All the other crap seemed silly to me—all the surface stuff about which architect was hot, and which architectural firm was the most cutting-edge, who was winning all the big architectural prizes, and blah, blah, blah. What I liked most was the building, the doing, the *making,* you know? Halfway through school I started to wonder if carpentry wasn't what I was made for. Man, I once made these bookshelves for this amazing house on the Cape, and I couldn't stop looking at them."

Mark looked at Paul and said, "I like creating something, you know? It feels good. That's the best I can explain it. But I'm not sure if that's a life."

"It's what you enjoy," said Paul. "What's wrong with that? Why not do what you enjoy? And who cares what everyone else is doing? Why not let all the surface stuff, as you call it, just fade away? Why not let go of all the comparisons and all the expectations about what's supposedly beneath you? Frankly, that's what we try to do here—strip things away so that we can be who we're called to be. It's like scraping off an old coat of paint from a table, so you can see the original wood. And usually what's underneath is more beautiful than we ever imagined."

Mark was still angry about making a pass at Anne, but this conversation had helped him cool down and shift perspective. He could feel his breathing slow down and muscles unclench, there in the breeze on the half-mowed lawn. Less embarrassed now, he pulled up the hem of his T-shirt and wiped his eyes.

"Why don't you let me see if we can give you the chance to do more carpentry work or other work that's a little more creative here?" said the abbot.

"Wow. That's really nice." He felt the need to shake Paul's hand, so he did.

"I hope you can see that your desire to be a carpenter may come from God. It may be a vocation for you. You're good at it. And in this case you can make a living doing what you love. So why not trust your desire?"

"Thanks," he said. He climbed back onto the lawnmower, switched on the ignition, and said, "Any advice about women?"

"Well," said Paul, crossing his arms, "you know what Jesus said."

"No!" said Mark, curious to hear dating advice from Jesus. Loudly, the lawnmower rumbled to life.

"There are plenty of fish in the sea!" said Paul over the noise of the engine.

"Jesus didn't say that!" said Mark over the now deafening roar.

"No!" said Paul, shouting at the top of his lungs. "But he should have!"

24

As Anne washed her dishes after a dinner of leftover salmon from a night out with Kerry, she thought about her prayer in the chapel from a few days before: "Are you there, God? It's me, Annie." It surprised her that she said the name that Father Edward still used, as if she were returning to a place she had once known or a person she had once been.

She looked over her shoulder at the photo of her baptism. The photo that Father Edward gave her was posted on the white refrigerator door, held there by the Phillies magnet. She remembered Jeremiah's own baptism, which was done grudgingly, out of respect for her parents, in what was supposedly her parish church, though she had never before set foot inside. "What's your parish?" her mother asked a few days after Jeremiah's birth and received a blank stare in response. Eddie was noncommittal. "Doesn't bother me if the priest splashes him with some water," he said when the topic was raised.

During Jeremiah's funeral, however, there came a moment when Anne was grateful that he had been baptized. The day before the funeral, she met with a priest at the local parish. The kind young Nigerian-born priest talked at length to her, but she forgot almost everything he said, because she could barely concentrate. But one comment made an impression.

"We place a cloth over his casket after it comes into the church," he said in heavily accented English, as they sat in a parlor crowded with heavy furniture. "Do you know what this symbolizes?" he asked.

She shook her head, unable to follow the conversation, so submerged was she in grief.

"It is called a pall," he said.

Anne was amazed that she hadn't known the derivation of the familiar word. *A pall was cast over him,* she thought. An avid reader, she must have come upon variations on that phrase dozens of times in novels. The pall represented the white clothes that infants wore at baptism. She wasn't sure she remembered the priest accurately, and the cloth that the funeral home used was almost as big as a tablecloth. But the symbolism made an impression on her. Anne wept hardest when the funeral director draped the long white cloth atop Jeremiah's casket after it was carried into the church by the pallbearers, another term she now understood. So at Jeremiah's funeral she thought about his baptism.

Her prayer the other night in the abbey chapel had confused her. She enjoyed it, but she wondered if it was even prayer. Once she introduced herself to God, she waited. And waited some more. What was supposed to happen? Was she supposed to say something else? Was she supposed to hear voices? She wished Father Paul were there to help her.

So she just sat with her eyes closed. It was so dark in the chapel that she couldn't see the image of Mary she liked, but she figured that closing her eyes was the right way to pray.

Almost immediately she thought about all the things she had to do over the next few days, and she felt her pulse quicken and her face flush. The audit that she and Kerry were working on was more complicated than either of them anticipated when they started the project. The client's financial records were a mess. She squeezed her eyes shut and grimaced.

Oh, to have more free time! *Ora et labora*? Isn't that what Maddy said the monks did? Was that "prayer and work"? Or was it "rest and work"? Either way, she longed for more rest in her life. But what would she do with free time? Spend more of it thinking about Jeremiah? Maybe it was better to work harder, to keep her mind off the past. Then again, with a little more free time, she could work in the garden . . .

Then she recalled the image of God as the gardener, the one she had talked with Paul about. He said it was a good image, so she decided it was okay to think about that.

Anne remembered the day in her backyard, when she knelt on the edge of the garden and had noticed the intense colors of the flowers. The reds and pinks and oranges came to her mind. The warmth of the sun on her neck. Her hands in the moist dirt. She pictured herself back in the garden now. She felt that calm again, and she relaxed. Comfort seemed to take root in her.

Then something strange happened. She wasn't sure if it was something she made up, but into her head, naturally and unexpectedly, came an image of Jesus walking in a garden.

Years ago, her Sunday school teacher had taught her class the song "Morning Has Broken." She remembered the sound of the roomful of students enthusiastically singing with their teacher. And there was one line of the song she liked especially. She still remembered it word for word: "Praise for the sweetness of the wet garden, sprung in completeness where his feet pass." As a girl, Anne liked to think about Jesus walking over dry land and leaving flowers in his footprints. She knew it probably didn't happen like that, but that's what she remembered as she sat in the chapel.

She enjoyed thinking about that image, and in her mind's eye could picture the orange and yellow marigolds left in Jesus's footprints. The colors were so bright, she could almost taste them: fresh orange juice and a lemon candy drop.

Then, all at once, another image came to her. Jesus was walking beside her in a beautiful garden, wearing her father's old gloves and her mother's gardening hat. What a strange image. It seemed as if they were walking near the tomb from which he rose on Easter Sunday. Sort of. She wasn't sure. But she felt happy to be with him, and because Paul told her that her first image was okay, she now allowed herself to think about this one: Jesus walking with her.

Anne inhaled, relaxed even more, and thought about that

for a long while. A minute passed. Then she wished that she could talk to him.

So she thought she would.

Anne said, *I miss him*.

She kept her eyes closed and waited.

Then in her imagination he said to her, *I know*.

She couldn't believe it. It seemed like a natural thing for him to say, as if he had been waiting to say it to her for a long time. It wasn't a vision or anything like that. And she certainly didn't hear it—like hearing the pew creak when she shifted. No, it was like something she thought of spontaneously, like in a daydream or an image that came into her mind when she was reading a novel. Jesus said it calmly too, almost as if it made him sad. He sounded a little bit like Father Paul and a little bit like her father. And a little bit like her mother too. Calm.

It frightened her a little, so she opened her eyes to reassure herself. She was still in the chapel, which was still dark, quiet, and, except for her, empty. When Anne closed her eyes again, she thought about what just happened and wondered if it was real, or made any sense, or was simply crazy. It was comforting, but also disturbing, and she opened her eyes again.

Anne passed her right hand over the smooth wood of the pew top in front of her and wondered how many people had come to this place seeking answers. She rubbed the top of the pew a few times, back and forth, and then stood, pulled the car keys from her pocket, and left the chapel.

Now tears sprang to her eyes when she remembered her time in the chapel. What did it all mean? Her hands still submerged in the warm soapy water, Anne turned to look at the photo of her baptism on the refrigerator and saw her white clothes, the same color that Jesus wore in the garden.

Then she heard a loud crack: a bat connecting with a baseball.

It was almost seven thirty. June was in full swing, and so were the boys in the neighborhood, playing baseball. She was amazed at the deep voices she heard through the closed window. When Jeremiah had died, his voice was just beginning to change. Those of his peers had continued on the journey toward manhood.

A solitary figure raced across her yard, picked up the stray ball, and yelled, "See ya!" to unseen friends in the yard next door. He trudged across her yard, head down, on his way home. Anne quickly opened the window over the sink and yelled out, "Brad!"

He froze and stared at her house as if it were a dangerous, living thing. Lightning bugs flickered around him in the darkness, and crickets sang. As he stood there, he remembered getting into trouble for turning a garden hose on that very window, after Jeremiah had dared him. They didn't know it was open, and Brad ended up getting water all over the kitchen floor. Jeremiah's mom was furious, but Jeremiah couldn't stop laughing, even after his mom flew out of the house, yelling at the both of them.

"Just a minute, Brad," Anne said from the window. And she disappeared from sight.

That night came back to Brad. Really it had never left.

It was just like tonight, sultry. After a long day of doing nothing (unless you counted playing video games, seeing who could make the blackest marks by skidding his bike to a halt on the sidewalk, and setting piles of dead leaves on fire with a magnifying glass), Brad, Jeremiah, and Gary wanted to see that movie on the first night it was out. Brad begged his parents to drive him, but they wouldn't. Neither would Jeremiah's mom. She didn't want Jeremiah to go at all. So Brad convinced the other two to ride their bikes up Germantown Pike, where they were forbidden to go because of the heavy traffic.

"Baby!" he yelled to Jeremiah, who was afraid to ride his bike anywhere near the highway.

Brad remembered all of it. They were late for the movie and needed to reach the other side of road quickly. Gary and Brad zipped across the four-lane highway easily, dodging cars and laughing as they did so.

"Come on!" he and Gary yelled at Jeremiah, daring him to cross. "Don't be such a *baby*!" They turned their backs.

What Brad remembered most was putting his right foot on the bike pedal, ready to push it down to propel his bike, and then hearing the bump, which sounded like someone had hit another car. When he turned around, his right foot still poised on the pedal, he saw someone lying in the street and a bike by the side of the road. Cars screeched to a halt on both sides of the highway, and by the time Brad reached the scene, the driver of the car was kneeling next to someone. When he saw his best friend, he threw up.

In tears, an hour later, after the ambulances and the police and their questions, Brad told his father and mother, though no one else, what he had done. Over and over his father and mother told him that it wasn't his fault, but he knew it was. He had decided they would go. He had convinced Jeremiah. He had told him to cross the street. He knew. He did it.

Brad didn't tell anyone how much he thought about Jeremiah. Not Gary, not his parents, not his teachers, not any of his friends in school. Not even the counselor the school hired to help him and the rest of his class after the accident.

After the funeral, he sat in a forking branch in the old crabapple tree in his back yard so that no one would see him. He cried so hard he thought he would choke.

He thought about J a lot. That's what they called each other: B and J. Those were names only the two of them used; no one else could, and only they knew that it wasn't "Bee" and "Jay," which wasn't cool. And there were no periods either, they had told Anne. Not B. and J. Just B and J.

No one knew this: he thought about J every day. When he played baseball, he thought of J, because he taught J the right way to hold a bat. ("How can you not *know* that, dude?" he said when he first saw J's crazy batting stance. J's face turned red, and Brad, instantly regretting his words, helped his friend adjust his hands on the bat.) When he was flipping through TV channels and caught their favorite cartoon in reruns, he thought of J. They used to watch that show on Saturday mornings with bowls of cereal on their laps and fall off the couch laughing about it, until J's mom made them shut it off. Now Brad thought the cartoon was pretty lame, but he watched it secretly sometimes. It was like being with J again, a little. When he passed the bus stop where they used to see who could spit the farthest, he thought of J. He didn't know if it was weird to think about someone who had been dead for three years, so he didn't tell anyone.

Brad looked at the house, terrified. J was still thirteen to him. He once asked his father whether, when he met J in heaven, he would be thirteen or grown up. Would J keep up with him? Or would Brad turn into a thirteen-year-old so that J could recognize him?

J's mom swung open the screen door. She was holding something by her side. Brad tensed up. He had avoided seeing her one-on-one for three years. Was she going to yell at him? As she walked over to him, Brad noticed that the crickets had stopped singing.

"How are you doing, Brad?" she said with a smile.

"Fine," he said quietly.

She could barely see his face in the dark, but the tone of his voice touched her with a deep sadness. When he looked at her, it was with an expression of either discomfort or fear— she couldn't tell. She was surprised to see stubble on his face, and she realized that Jeremiah would probably look like this too. Brad was now taller than Anne. Imagine.

"I hear you're driving now," she said.

Brad grinned slightly. "Yeah, I got my license the other day. It's pretty cool to be able to drive. I wish . . ."

He stopped. A lightning bug landed on the front of his shirt and blinked its tail once.

"I wish I could tell J," he said, seeming as surprised to say it as she was to hear it.

"You were a good friend to him," she said.

Brad fixed his eyes on the ground. Anne could sense his discomfort, even the need to escape this conversation.

"I miss him," he said, blinking back tears. Then he said, "I think about him a lot."

"Me too."

The lightning bug lit up the front of his shirt.

"You know," said Anne. "I don't think I ever told you what Jeremiah said about you a few days before the accident. He said that you were the funnest person he ever knew. I think that's a really great compliment."

Brad stared at his sneakers. "Mmm hmm."

"So I wanted to give you this," she said, holding out a baseball glove with a letter "J" written in black magic marker on the outside of the thumb.

Brad put the baseball he was carrying into his pocket, wiped his hands on his shorts, took the glove from Anne, and said nothing. Then he slipped his hand inside the glove.

"Thanks," he said. As he looked at J's glove, his mouth turned down, his head dropped, his lips tightened almost to the point of turning white, and he began crying in earnest. Brad made no sound, but in the silence Anne could hear the tears falling onto his T-shirt. Anne grabbed him before he could say anything and hugged him tight. She noticed how tall he was and wondered if Jeremiah would have been as tall as his father. The question made her squeeze her eyes shut.

She thought she would cry, but she felt only calm. After a few moments she released him, because she knew enough about teenage boys to know that he was probably uncomfortable.

"Thanks . . . for the glove," he said, head still bowed.

"Thanks for being such a good friend to J."

She smiled, turned, and walked back toward her house.

After the screen door slammed, Brad remained in the yard, wiped his tears with his right hand, and blew his nose on the bottom of his T-shirt. He looked at J's house. Then he opened and closed his hand inside the glove, put his face to the old leather, and inhaled. It smelled like his past.

25

"You've been a big help to Annie," said Father Edward to Father Paul, who was glad that the old priest was finally out of the infirmary wing and back in his dormitory room.

Paul sat on a wooden chair in Edward's room, where he was seeking some advice. Paul often used his former novice director as a sounding board.

In the twenty-five years since Paul had been in the novitiate, Edward had changed. All of his former novices said so. As novice director, Edward had been a formidable man: austere, rigid, and even harsh. But age and a bout with cancer ten years ago had mellowed him. Now the community saw him as a cheerful, relaxed, and at times playful man. Thanks to age, experience, and the workings of grace, Edward was the freest man Paul had ever met.

"Thanks," said Paul. "Occasionally I'm not sure how to approach Anne. I've counseled people who are grieving, of course, but usually not someone so doubtful about God. So I sometimes feel off-kilter. The other day I suggested that she do some imaginative contemplation, and imagine herself talking to God, and you should have seen the look on her face. It's a delicate balance, as you know. I don't want to force her toward a belief that may not be natural to her. At the same time, God's really working in her. So I'm just praying that I give her freedom and help her see God's invitation."

"Well, remember," he said. "Spirituality is like spaghetti."

Paul suppressed a smile. He had heard this analogy many times in the novitiate, but he let his old novice director offer it again.

"When my mother, may she rest in peace, cooked spaghetti, she used to throw a few strands against the kitchen wall. When it stuck, she said it was done. It's the same in the spiritual life. Not every homily you preach or insight you offer will stick. A lot depends on where the person is, whether they're open to hearing what you have to say, and whether it's the right time for them to hear it. One day you say something that you think is profound, and they just shrug. A few months later, you say the same thing, and they start crying. Who knows? In other words, a lot of it depends on grace. Maybe all of it."

Paul agreed. He had given enough homilies and counseled enough monks to know that the most offhand comment sometimes seemed to the hearer the wisest thing ever said, and insights that Paul deemed helpful could leave a monk more confused than when he had come into the abbot's office.

"Thanks," he said. "It's a blessing to be with Anne. And I won't break confidence, but it's been wonderful that the two of you have reconnected. Imagine your having baptized her all those years ago."

"A blessing for me too," said Edward. "I had always wondered whatever had become of her. And it was a grace to be reminded of my, um, more active days." Laboriously rising from his easy chair, he made his way to his bookcase.

Father Edward had more mementoes than most monks at P&J, and technically the monks' cells were not supposed to be crammed with possessions, but Paul allowed the older members of the community more latitude.

"Her parents were wonderful," he said, poking through an old shoebox on his bookshelf. "Just wonderful."

A yellowing photo was fished out of the shoebox and handed to the abbot. It showed a smiling man with a full head of gray hair sitting at the abbot's desk. He wore a white button-down shirt, with its sleeves rolled up, and a tie at half-mast. Surrounded by a pile of papers and an old calculator, he was apparently poring over the monastery's accounts. Paul grinned when he realized that the furniture in the abbot's office was precisely the same as it is today.

"That's something," said Paul. "Her father?"

"Mmm hmm," said Edward. "And a good friend to me."

Edward proffered another photo of a young couple with a small child standing outside the abbey church. The mother, looking squarely at the camera, held the child in her arms, who reached out to grab three fingers on her father's hand. "That's Annie's mother of course. Very sweet woman. They were a great couple."

"Her mother had a huge heart, and she was also quite lovely, as you can see," said Edward. "And Annie is just as lovely, I think."

Paul remembered how she looked the other day: tanned and fit, wearing a tailored white shirt and khaki pants that showed off a slim figure. Occasionally, Paul felt attracted to women he met, but it rarely bothered him. It was simply part of life. He reminded himself that he'd feel this way if he were a married man who was attracted to a coworker.

Only once during his monastic life had Paul fallen deeply in love—with a woman he met at a Catholic college in Minnesota during a weeklong conference on, of all things, monasticism. She was a bright academic, recently divorced, roughly his age, and it was easy to fall into conversation with her. After a few laughter-filled meals together, Paul realized that he was falling in love. After the conference ended and Paul returned to the monastery and she to her university job in Ohio, the two carried on a correspondence. Within a few months, she wrote him a letter confessing that she had strong feelings for him.

Paul never told her about his own attraction, because he felt such a disclosure would lead her to think there was a future in the relationship. Even with a good deal of self-knowledge and a few hundred miles between them, the relationship proved a challenge for Paul. In the end, he reminded himself of the life he had chosen and how happy he was as a monk. In a letter to her, Paul told her how grateful he was for her friendship, but also that writing so frequently probably wasn't a good idea for either of them. A few years later, when she remarried, Paul found himself relieved. Now they exchanged Christmas cards.

As abbot, Paul also knew of the occasional monk who had fallen in love with another monk. That was a more difficult situation, given the challenges of proximity. Usually things worked themselves out when the monks focused on the rest of the community, found satisfaction in their work and prayer, and were able to put some emotional distance between themselves. Sometimes, though, it didn't work out, and one or both monks ended up leaving.

Since he was speaking with his former novice director, Paul figured it couldn't hurt to mention what was on his mind. "That's a little bit of a challenge for me when it comes to Anne."

"You know the old saying," Edward said, sinking back into his chair. "Those feelings don't go away until ten minutes after we're dead. As long as we acknowledge those feelings and remind ourselves that as monks we don't have to act on them, we'll be okay. And it's important to talk about this with God in your prayer. I'm sure I told you this a thousand years ago in the novitiate, but those feelings show you that you're alive."

Father Edward then shrugged his shoulders and said, "It's a struggle sometimes of course. But what life doesn't have struggles? The key is love. As long as your chastity helps you to love, you're okay. Because that's all God asks from us here. To love."

Paul was grateful for the encouragement. Spending time with his old novice director also reminded him of the time when he was still in his "first fervor," as the monks called it: right after he entered, when he still thought that the monastery was perfect. After a year, the honeymoon ended, as it did in every relationship. Then Paul saw the monastery as it was—a place where people tried to live holy lives, but a place that was no less mixed up than any other human community. Reconnecting with the basics of his vocation—why he entered, what drew him here, what the vows meant—always rekindled his youthful ardor, which helped him in his current life.

"Plus," said Edward, "you've been a big help to Annie. So why not just relax?"

Paul nodded, grateful for the advice.

"So, Ed, I'm off to meet with her now. Pray for us."

"Oh," he said, "I've been doing that since she came back to us."

After the abbot gave Father Edward his blessing, he left his room. On the way to his office, he passed the cloister garden. He had a few minutes before his meeting with Anne, so he decided to sit on the bench and enjoy the view, which since becoming abbot he had not had as much time to do.

The small white blossoms from the dogwood trees had been gone for several days, as had the puffy pink blossoms of the cherry trees, but the red roses were in full bloom now, and around the stone paths purple snapdragons swayed on their pale green stalks. Early in the spring, Brother Stephen, the monk in charge of the monastery gardens, had planted impatiens around the border of the stone paths, which Paul initially disliked. Too gaudy, he had thought. But tonight he revised his earlier prejudice: the pillowy bunches of reds and oranges and pinks were lovely in the waning sunshine. A blue jay cried out from the branches of one of the dogwood trees.

There were some unexpected perks of being abbot. Paul always was partial to purple phlox and snapdragons, flowers that he remembered from his mother's garden, so he asked Brother Stephen to plant some of both in the cloister garden, and Stephen said he was delighted to do it. "Your predecessor," laughed Stephen, "couldn't tell a rosebush from a maple tree." Emboldened, the next year Paul mentioned planting some lilac bushes, which now exploded in color and scent every year and attracted a surfeit of tiger swallowtails.

All the flowers looked marvelous together, the ones he didn't care for and the ones he did. His appreciation was intensified by his cheerful mood, lightened by his talk with his old novice director, and encouraged by knowing that he would soon see God at work in Anne. *Yes,* he thought, *the cloister garden looks especially lovely tonight.*

How beautiful the world looks when things make sense.

26

Anne was waiting for Paul in the abbot's office. More comfortable now at the monastery, she had also become friendly with Maddy in the guest house. "You know the way," Maddy had said when she arrived early for her meeting with Paul.

"I come bearing gifts," she said, standing up from her chair.

"Thank you," said the abbot. "How lovely!" He was carrying a large red book, with multicolored ribbons flowing from between its pages, which he placed on his desk.

Anne held out a green plastic planter overflowing with purple-and-white petunias. "They're from my garden. They're coming in really well this year." Through the office doorway, Anne glanced into the cloister garden. "But I guess bringing flowers here is like bringing you jam. Looks like you have more than enough of both."

"But these are from you. We don't have any of those. And it will remind us of you and remind us to pray for you."

Anne was amazed by how Paul could so gracefully turn something awkward into something beautiful.

"I have something weird I need to ask you about," she said, as she sat down in the wingback chair. She flicked a piece of lint off the arm of the chair. "Oh, I'm sorry, that was rude," she said. "First of all, how are you?"

"No, not at all. I'm fine. What did you want to ask me?"

"I had this strange experience in the chapel the other night. Remember when we were talking about images of God? My thinking about God patting down the soil and your talking about Jesus the gardener?"

Paul nodded. "Yes, very well."

"Well, after we talked, I went into the chapel and sat in one of the pews. I wasn't sure what to do, since I'm not much for prayer. So, anyway, I was just quiet for a bit. And I started to think about that idea of Jesus as the gardener. So I'm sitting there and . . ."

She paused.

Paul said, "Keep going."

"This is going to sound weird," said Anne.

"I'll bet it doesn't sound weird to me at all."

"So I'm sitting there . . . and all of a sudden I thought of this song I liked when I was going to Sunday school, or whatever it's called now. We used to sing this song, 'Morning Has Broken.' Do you know that one? It was pretty popular back in the day."

"Of course." Paul started to sing in a soft baritone, "Morning has broken, like the first morning. Blackbird has spoken, like the first bird . . ."

"Yeah, that's it," said Anne. "Hey, you've got a nice voice."

Paul smiled slightly. "It's more or less required here."

Anne laughed quickly and continued, "Anyway I used to love that line, 'Praise for the sweetness of the wet garden, sprung in completeness where his feet pass.' In fact, I asked my mom if it ever really happened, and she said that anything was possible. When I was little I used to think about Jesus walking across the desert, in Nazareth or Galilee or wherever. I'm not even sure if there's a desert there, but I used to think of flowers springing up in his footprints in the dry ground. So anyway, I'm sitting in the chapel, and suddenly I have that image in my head of Jesus—walking across the dry ground and leaving flowers behind. It just sort of popped into my mind. And here's the weird thing: he's wearing my mom's gardening hat—the one that I wear—and my dad's gloves—the ones I use now."

Anne shook her head. "It was weird. It was so vivid. Not like I was having a vision or anything. I didn't see him standing in the chapel or anything like that. More like it just came into my mind. On its own. But it was really beautiful. I had never had anything like that happen. It was nice, though. Is that normal?"

Paul smiled. "Yes it is. It's not something that happens every day, but these kinds of experiences are fairly common for people once they start praying. And it's a real gift when they happen. Did anything else come up?"

"Well," she said, "I felt like talking to him so I said, 'I miss him.' And then he said . . ."

Anne paused and looked down at her white dress shirt and red linen pants.

Paul waited.

"He said . . . 'I know.'" Anne's voice quavered. She could remember that moment so clearly now.

"It was so beautiful," she said. "It was like he really *did* know. And he really did feel sad for me. And just now, as we're sitting here, I'm remembering that question you asked me about how Jesus felt. Now I feel like he really felt sorry for me."

She looked at the abbot then. "I'm not sure what to think about this. Is this crazy?"

"No, not at all. It's the opposite of crazy."

"So is this all in my mind, or did it really happen?"

"Why not both?" said Paul. "God can work through your imagination. How else would God come to you in prayer? After all, he made your imagination. And you know what? Jesus *does* feel sorry for you. And 'feeling sorry' really doesn't go far enough. Jesus feels *with* you. He has compassion for you."

Anne thought about times when she knew that another person wasn't just patting her on the shoulder, feeling pity for her, but remaining there with her in the middle of the pain. There was a big difference.

"I've never experienced anything like this—the prayer, I mean."

"Maybe God's been waiting for the right moment to come to you in this way," said Paul. "And I think it's beautiful. Can you trust in all this?"

"I think I have to trust that I'm not losing my mind."

"Well, if you are," said Paul, "then all the saints and everyone else who has ever had any experiences in prayer are out of their minds too. Including me."

"Does that kind of thing happen in prayer a lot?"

"All sorts of things happen in prayer," said Paul. "The kind of images you experienced are just one way that God comes to us. For some people it's mainly emotions that come up—like joy or contentment when they're thinking about God. Other people have memories that bubble up, maybe from childhood, and they feel it heals them in some way. Or it reminds them how much God loved them even when they were young. Sometimes it's just an insight—like figuring something out about a problem that's been bugging you. All those things can happen. Then sometimes it seems like nothing is coming up. That can be pretty frustrating. But in those times we have to trust that God is doing some work deep within us. Because any time spent in God's presence is transformative. But really our main work in prayer is simply to be present to God and open ourselves up. 'Show up and shut up,' as one of the monks here likes to say."

Anne listened.

"But, yes, what you talk about happens. The question is, do you believe that this is God speaking with you and telling you that he cares? Can you believe it's real?"

Anne looked out the window at the darkening sky. All day she had looked forward to her meeting with Paul. At lunch, Kerry teased Anne after she admitted how much she enjoyed her visits to the abbey. "Dear Sister Anne," she wrote in an e-mail later in the day. "When you join the convent, please remember to send me some free jam."

It didn't make any sense—Anne obviously wasn't joining any convent, and there were no women here anyway. But she found it funny and wrote back, "May God bless you, my daughter."

How had she come to this place, where a monk was asking her if she believed in God's presence in her life? Was it by chance that her car had broken down and Mark brought her here that night in the rainstorm? Would she have felt comfortable calling Mark if he hadn't stopped by the day before to tell her about the broken window and the baseball? She thought about her talk with Brad and the look on his face when she gave him the baseball glove. She was glad that she was able to comfort him after all this time.

Then, sitting in Paul's office, she remembered a moment in Jeremiah's life she had long forgotten: when he told her about his first hit in Little League. She hadn't been there to see it— and that's when she promised herself that she would never miss another game—but hearing him describe what it was like to connect with the ball and make it to first base seemed sweeter than being there to see it. The look on Jeremiah's face was that of absolute delight. Joy radiated from him when he told her the story. It was this memory that returned to her now.

Anne felt lighter—like something new was opening up for her. It wasn't that she wasn't still sad about Jeremiah or didn't want him back. More than anything she wanted him back.

And it wasn't that she still wasn't angry at God. But she felt something else too. Anne felt that God was with her that day in the garden. She did. She felt that God felt compassion for her. She really did. She couldn't deny that.

So she said, "Yes. I think I can believe that."

"I'm glad," said Paul, leaning back in his chair. "Because that's the first step in prayer: trusting that these things that happen to you are coming from God. Think about it—how else would God come to us? Most of the time God comes to us through everyday things—like relationships and work and family and friends. But sometimes, as you found out in your garden and in the chapel, God comes to us in very personal ways. And you know what's great? It's tailor-made for you, Anne. God uses things from your life to speak to you—your love of gardening, your mom's hat, your dad's gloves. It's sort of like the parables."

"Excuse me?"

"Sorry," he said, smiling. "I get a little carried away sometimes." He removed his glasses to wipe away some dust with the hem of his black scapular. "What I meant was that in the parables Jesus used things from people's everyday lives—like birds and seeds and clouds and things that people in his time were familiar with—and he turned them into stories to help them understand God's love. The same thing happens in our own lives. God uses familiar things to help us understand God's love for us. God speaks to you in ways you, Anne, can understand, using things from your life, things you love, to meet you where you are. It never fails to amaze me."

202 ❖ James Martin, SJ

"I'm not sure where to go with all this," said Anne.

"Why not let God take the lead? Why not just be open to the ways that God wants to be with you?"

"Okay," she said, exhaling. "But I still miss Jeremiah."

"Of course you do. And you always will. But now I'll say something that I didn't want to say at the beginning, because I thought you might take it the wrong way. I wonder if it helps you to know that Jeremiah is with Jesus the gardener. The same person who met you in prayer is the one who welcomed your son with open arms into heaven."

Anne's head dropped when she heard that.

"Maybe I shouldn't have said that," Paul said. "But I believe that."

Anne could see the church's steeple through the leaves outside, and she remembered her father's words, about it rising like a ship's mast slowly coming over the horizon.

"I think I do too," she said.

The bell rang for Compline.

"Oh!" said Paul. "I'm always surprised by those bells, even after twenty-five years." He stood and straightened his scapular. "Would you like to join us?"

"Why not?" she said.

27

Mark was grateful that Anne had allowed him to turn the garage into a workshop. By the end of the summer, he had finished clearing out the trash that had accumulated from Anne's two previous tenants, painted the cinder-block walls a glossy white, and installed new lighting, all of which Anne appreciated. It wasn't as elegant a workshop as the one Mark's mentor had in Cambridge, but it was a good beginning.

Over the past few weeks, Mark had squirreled away enough money to purchase the basic carpentry tools, which now hung on pegboards, which he had painted white and nailed to the garage wall. His truck could withstand the elements in the summer, so there was plenty of workspace inside the garage. And he did not lack for business. Attracted by the apparently irresistible noise of hammering and sawing, the boys on his block had already poked their heads into the garage several times, which ensured that their parents would know what Mark was doing and that jobs would follow. Brad took a particular interest in the workshop and had started dropping by to examine Mark's tools and talk with him about cars, and girls.

"Maybe I'm not the best one to give you advice on girls," he said to Brad one Saturday afternoon in late August. Mark was sanding a small pine bookshelf he had designed to sit atop Father Paul's cluttered desk. It was going to be a surprise. He was grateful for the advice Paul had offered over the past few months and figured this would be a good way to say thanks.

"Are you kidding?" said Brad, who sat on the concrete floor, cross-legged, looking up at the carpenter. "I saw that girl you went out with a few months ago. The tall one? With the Mercedes? She was hot!"

"That's not always the most important thing in the world—hot, I mean." When Brad eyes widened, as if in a cartoon, Mark laughed.

"Let me show you the right way to sand," he said. "That may be easier to learn."

In the past few weeks, Father Paul had fulfilled his promise to find Mark more carpentry work at the abbey. Already Mark had completed a small oak table to hold a vase of flowers that stood next to a picture of Mary in the chapel. The old metal table was too rickety—it threatened to topple every time someone's habit brushed against it—so Mark offered to build a replacement. Whenever he passed the chapel, he paused to stare at the new table, slender but solid.

"Pride is one of the seven deadly sins, you know," said Brother Robert with a sly grin when he saw Mark's gaze linger on the new table.

Anne was pleased that Mark had refurbished the garage, since she had never found the time to clean it out. She also respected Mark's carpentry skills and was happy to help him in his work. She could tell Mark was still interested in her romantically, but she remained uninterested in dating a frat boy—even a kind one. Still, she was glad to support Mark. He seemed to appreciate this romantic détente and treated her with a guarded but noticeable affection.

When Anne asked how much she owed for the paint and repairs on the garage, he shook his head.

"You're helping me out, so it'll cost you nothing. The best things in life are free."

That was the same thing Father Paul told Anne when she offered to pay him for what she came to realize were spiritual direction sessions. (She had read that nomenclature on a flyer that she had picked up in the guest house.) Nonetheless, she made an anonymous donation to the monastery. Secretly she was delighted when the abbot told her what a blessing it was that someone had given funds to help renovate the chapel. The first thing he would do, he said, would be to replace the old metal table next to the portrait of Mary.

Anne's life had changed over the summer, which she ascribed not only to the workings of time, but to time at the abbey. Father Paul's expression grew serious when she told him this a few days ago, after she stopped by with more flowers.

"It wasn't the abbey that did this for you," he said. "It was God."

"Well," Anne said, "if I hadn't come to the abbey, none of this would have happened."

"And who do you think brought you to the abbey?"

Anne started to say "Mark," but realized what Paul was driving at. So she just laughed. She still was angry with God for taking away Jeremiah. And she still had a hard time believing God was behind every good thing that happened. *But maybe*, she thought, *behind some good things.*

The photos of Jeremiah on her living room wall would stay. In fact, she added a few new ones. Beside Jeremiah's final school picture, she hung a photo of his baptism that her mom had taken. Anne had dug it out of a box in her garage she had thought was lost and framed it to match the school photo she liked so much. Anne and her husband were holding their tiny son—who was screaming at top volume—and beaming. Her parents, standing behind them, wore, she admitted ruefully, small self-satisfied grins on their faces. But, she figured, they probably had the same look now in heaven as well, having seen her spend so much time at the abbey. Anne wasn't ready to start going to Mass—still too busy—but she felt that it might be a possibility, sometime.

Next to the photo of Jeremiah's baptism was the photo of her own baptism, which Father Edward had given her. She had given Father Edward a framed copy as well, which he set on his desk. A few days ago he told her he prayed for Jeremiah and her every night.

28

One Sunday night toward the end of the summer at the Abbey of Saints Philip and James in suburban Philadelphia, the bell rang to announce Compline. The monks entered the church wordlessly and after making deep bows toward the altar filed into their seats. The twenty or so monks looked like unremarkable men. Take them out of their long black-and-white habits, and they could have been accountants or lawyers or plumbers or teachers or carpenters.

The abbot, a thin, middle-aged man wearing large black glasses, rapped a knuckle of his right hand on the wooden stall to signal that prayers were to begin. Next to the abbot was an older monk, stooped but with a full head of gray hair, who had parked his metal walker beside the stall.

The sun was setting, and the thick stained-glass windows admitted no light. Instead, the church itself was the source of light, and from outside the windows glowed a deep blue, almost violet.

"Let my evening prayer ascend before you, O Lord," sang the presider.

"And may your loving-kindness descend upon us," answered the rest of the monks.

In the rear of the church a scattering of six people sat in the visitors' section. An older woman, a widow who had been coming to the monastery for several years, drawn by the physical beauty of the place. A college student who was thinking about becoming a priest or a monk, but was still years from deciding. A middle-aged couple, professors from a nearby college, both agnostic, who enjoyed the singing. In the back, closest to the door, sat two more people.

One was the abbey's handyman and carpenter. According to the abbey's phone directory, he was officially "Director of the Physical Plant." Normally Sunday was his day off, but he had come by to finish staining a pair of maple bookcases he had built for the library. It was his most ambitious carpentry job yet, but he enjoyed the work.

The carpenter, a tall man with long sandy hair, was always welcome to the monastery prayers, but he seldom came. Tonight, however, with the summer drawing to a close and the weather turning cooler, the world had seemed so beautiful. A few hours earlier, as he was staining the shelves, he felt a sudden burst of contentment, of rightness, as if this was where he was supposed to be. Not much had changed in his life this summer, he had to admit. He still hadn't found the right woman, as he had been hoping. But he was a little bit happier in his work. So he wanted to thank God. The man took off his sweat-stained Red Sox cap after he entered the church, sat in an empty pew, and closed his eyes.

Three rows behind him sat a tanned, middle-aged woman in a Phillies T-shirt and faded jeans. The carpenter couldn't see her, nor would she tell the carpenter that she was there until a few days later, and they would both laugh about it. She had spent an enjoyable day weeding her garden and cooking a relaxing dinner for a friend from work. Just a few minutes before, she had visited the elderly monk with the walker, who had been a friend of her father and mother.

Were you to see this woman, you might wonder what brought her. You might suspect that she was a devout Catholic. Who else would spend a Sunday evening at a monastery? But she wasn't. She was far from what anyone would call a churchgoer and couldn't remember the last time she had attended Mass. You might think she had been coming here for years and so knew the monastery well. But that wouldn't describe her either. She knew only a handful of the monks. You might guess that she was a kind of spiritual tourist, sampling this tradition and that, having recently discovered monasticism, she might move on once her interest waned. But that also wasn't accurate. Her attraction went deeper. Finally, you might conclude that she was a lost soul, lacking any real connections in her life. But you'd be wrong about that too. She felt connected to her friends, to her late son, and now, in a new way, to her faith, or at least *a* faith. Like most people, she couldn't be categorized easily.

Were you to look more carefully, though, you would see one thing clearly. As the monks sang their final prayer of the day, her gaze was drawn to an image of Mary holding Jesus, which stood on a table against a side wall of the church. Next to that table was a smaller wooden one, on which was placed a vase filled with purple snapdragons. The woman looked at the image several times during Compline.

You would also see that she was singing along with the monks. It was a song that her father used to sing, one that she had forgotten for a long time.

But now she knew the words, by heart.

Acknowledgments

This novel is based on a dream. So the characters of Anne, Mark, and Paul are not based on real-life individuals, except perhaps unconsciously. Also, although the conversations between the characters are grounded in experiences I've had as a spiritual director and as someone who has received spiritual direction, none is based on any one person or situation. Anne's experiences, struggles, and questions are common in the spiritual life—as are Mark's and Paul's. Finally, the Abbey of Saints Philip and James is not a real place, but flows from my experiences with Trappist and Benedictine monks and monasteries in the United States.

I would like to thank readers of an early version of this manuscript who generously offered their helpful suggestions: Jim Keane; Ron Hansen; Kathleen Norris; William A. Barry, SJ; Janice Farnham, RJM; Kerry Weber; Dan Pawlus; Louise Murray; Liza Fiol-Matta; Paul Mariani; and James Palmigiano, OCSO. Thanks to a humble editor of this manuscript who wants to remain anonymous, but who improved the book immeasurably with her edits, comments, additions, and advice. Thanks to Joseph McAuley for cheerfully helping to input all the edits. Thanks to Heidi Hill, for checking all the facts and making sure the flowers bloomed in the right order. And at HarperOne, thanks to Roger Freet and Michael Maudlin for their encouragement and support, and to Noël Chrisman and Ann Moru for their wonderful care for the manuscript.

Most of all, thanks to God for the dream, and for everything else.

Reading and Discussion Guide

1. As Mark goes about his duties as director of the physical plant at the abbey, Father Paul often reminds him that Jesus was a carpenter (p. 24). How does the way Mark feels about this comment evolve over the course of the book?

2. Anne was never a religious person but seems to experience a dramatic loss of faith following her son's death. Have you had an experience that made you question your faith? Why does loss in particular make us feel distant from or frustrated with God?

3. Early on, Mark seems to fear Anne, worrying about how she will react to the news of the broken window and calling her a "stickler" for certain things. How do you feel about Anne?

4. Something Anne disliked about church was "people were always telling you what not to do" (p. 42). Do you have similar feelings about your religious denomination? Why might Anne or others have this impression?

5. Father Paul describes Mark to Anne as "a holy man . . . in his own way" (p. 51). What do you think he means? Does

Mark seem "holy" to you? What qualities make someone
holy? Who around you would you characterize as a holy
man or holy woman?

6. Why do you think Anne is so drawn to the portrait of the
Virgin Mary? What does Mary represent for Anne?

7. Father Paul, reflecting on life in the monastery, thinks
about how he has become less concerned about spiritual
dry patches. "Perhaps," he thinks, "the human heart
couldn't take it if God were always so close" (p. 61). Have
you ever hit spiritual dry patches in your life? Do his
words ring true?

8. Father Paul recalls the reaction of his friends when he
first entered the novitiate. "They thought either that Paul
was wasting his life . . . or that he was entering a perfect
world where strife was unknown, mortal problems were
banished, and a rich prayer life was the norm" (p. 59). Has
reading *The Abbey* changed the way you feel about monastic life? What do you find appealing about such a life?
What do you think would be a struggle?

9. Father Paul thinks often of a quote from Saint John
Berchmans, which Paul translates as "life in community is
my greatest penance" (pp. 64–65). How do you understand
this statement? What aspects of life in community might
make it a penance?

10. On page 98, Anne explains her old image of God as "this
person in the sky who's judging me every minute of the

day. Looking at everything I do—all the times I didn't go to Mass, all the times I got angry after Jeremiah's death, and all the times that I got pissed off at my ex-husband—and ticking off everything in little boxes that say 'Right' and 'Wrong.' " How does her image of God change over the course of the book? How have your images of God changed throughout your life?

11. When Anne shares with Father Paul her feelings about Jeremiah's death, she admits that she told God, "I hate you." Paul responds that her prayer was a good one (p. 116). Why does he consider that a good prayer? Does such a sentiment surprise you? What do you think God desires most from us in our prayers?

12. According to Father Paul, "Monastic life made it easier to find God" (p. 119), although he does not think that monks are holier than other people. In fact, he thinks "the opposite was more often true" (p. 119). Why does he think those who live outside the monastery are holier than monks? Do you agree? Why or why not?

13. When Anne writes the letter to God, she is surprised that it expresses more sadness than anger (p. 129). If you wrote a letter to God today, what might it say? What experiences would it describe? What emotions would it express?

14. Anne lists her "sanity-preserving measures" (p. 131): gardening, dinners with her co-worker, yoga classes, talking

on the phone with her college roommate, going to work every day, and long walks by the river. What would be on your list?

15. When Anne tells her friend and co-worker Kerry about the time she's been spending at the abbey, Kerry worries that Anne will become a religious "fanatic" (p. 141). Have you ever been afraid to talk about faith or spirituality with a friend or co-worker for fear that person would have a similar reaction?

16. Father Paul tells Anne that our images of God often come from the way our parents treated us (p. 145). How have your parents, or other authority figures, influenced the way you see God?

17. When Father Paul confesses to Father Edward that he is attracted to Anne, Edward replies, "It's a struggle sometimes of course. But what life doesn't have struggles? The key is love. As long as your chastity helps you to love, you're okay. Because that's all God asks from us here. To love" (p. 191). Does it surprise you to learn that monks might struggle with such things? Why or why not?

18. Father Paul reflects, "How beautiful the world is when things make sense" (p. 193). What does this mean to you?

19. What do you make of Anne and Mark's relationship? How do they grow together in their friendship and their faith journeys? How do you think their relationship might evolve?

20. Reflecting on the idea of Jesus as gardener, Anne has a surprising experience of Jesus in which he is wearing her mom's gardening hat and her dad's gloves (p. 197). Father Paul tells her God uses familiar things from our lives to tell us of God's love for us (p. 201). What things in your life has God chosen to speak to you through?

21. Have you ever had an experience that is similar to Anne's? That is, have you ever felt God communicating with you directly?

22. Over the course of the book, Anne learns something not only about the spiritual life but about prayer. What is prayer for you?

23. As the book comes to a close, many things remain the same. Mark is still working for the monastery; he has still not found the right woman. Yet how has his life changed? How has Anne's?

24. Has your image of God changed after reading this book? If so, how?

25. Which character from *The Abbey* do you identify with most? Whose faith journey is most familiar to you? Has anything in this book shed light on faith, God, or perhaps life, in a new way? If so, what?

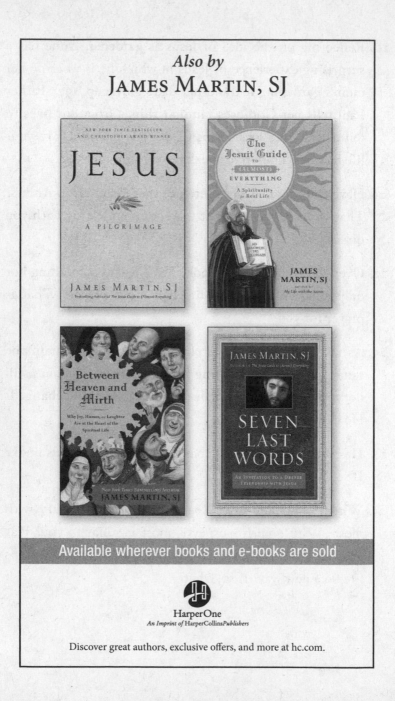